Royal
Botanic Garden
Edinburgh

Wych Elm

Mary Beith

Max Coleman

Brian Coppins

Ian Edwards

Stephan Helfer

Peter Toaig

Roy Watling

Edited by

Max Coleman

With kind support from

Forestry Commission
Scotland

Scottish
Arts Council

**SCOTTISH
NATURAL
HERITAGE**

Maturing fruits produce the first flush of green on wych elm during spring, Ballachulish, Highland. Image: Michael Brooks.

First published by the

Royal
Botanic Garden
Edinburgh

20A Inverleith Row, Edinburgh EH3 5LR, UK

ISBN: 978-1-906129-21-7 Paperback edition
ISBN: 978-1-906129-25-5 Hardback edition

The Royal Botanic Garden Edinburgh (RBGE) confirms that all addresses,
contact details and URLs of websites are accurate at the time of going to press.
RBGE cannot be responsible for details which become out of date after publication.

Every effort has been made to trace holders of copyright in text and illustrations.
Should there be any inadvertent omissions or errors the publishers will be pleased to correct them for future editions.

Printed by Scotprint, Scotland

Cover image: Wych elm grain reproduced life size with calligraphy by Susie Leiper and wood prepared by Roger Hall.

The Garden's wych elm in charcoal
and chalk by Kate Downie.

4 seasons.

Wych Elm

the branches fall away from the stem
like water tumbling over rocks
cascade

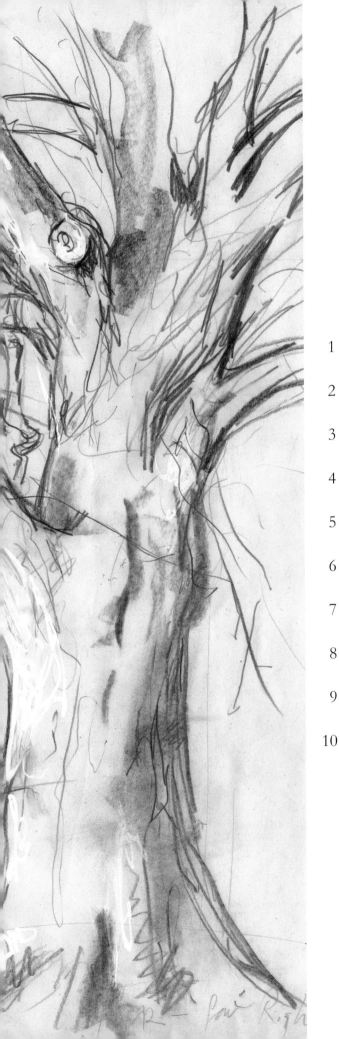

Contents

Foreword   7
Professor Stephen Blackmore FRSE
Regius Keeper
Royal Botanic Garden Edinburgh

Foreword   9
Dr Bob McIntosh FICFor, FRICS
Director
Forestry Commission Scotland

1 | A Highly Prized Tree   11

2 | Elm of the Brae   19

3 | A Very Tantalising Tree   29

4 | Versatility and Utility   39

5 | Something to Sit On   49

6 | Death, Decay and New Life   55

7 | Grim Reaper   63

8 | Phoenix Tree   71

9 | Celebrating a Life   77

10 | Meet the Makers   85

Contact details   133

Biographies   135

Bibliography   139

Acknowledgements   143

Index   145

6

Wych elm canopy in winter.
Image: RBGE/Max Coleman.

Foreword

The wych elm is a native tree that colonised Scotland after the glaciers of the last Ice Age had retreated and long before people bent its branches into bows or turned its timber into wheels. The devastating impact of Dutch elm disease since the 1970s has meant that the north and west of Scotland are now regarded as among the last bastions of the wych elm in Europe. Even there it is now threatened by climate change which might bring the milder conditions more favourable to the spread of the disease. Despite its status as a distinctive and widespread member of the Scottish tree flora wych elm is not used to define any particular woodland type and is rarely mentioned as a particularly Scottish tree. Lacking the iconic status of pine, oak or birch, it seems that wych elm is a forgotten tree, an oversight this book, the first dedicated to this quintessentially Scottish tree, aims to redress.

This book, produced with the support of Forestry Commission Scotland, covers the natural history, folklore and uses of wych elm, with a special emphasis on its importance in Scotland. It was conceived as part of a wider project launched when an ancient wych elm that grew at the Edinburgh Garden of the Royal Botanic Garden Edinburgh succumbed to disease in 2003. At that point the tree might simply have been destroyed by burning or chipping but Ian Edwards envisaged the possibility of giving it new life by inviting a variety of craftspeople to create individual pieces from the beautiful wood. The resulting work forms the opening exhibition in the John Hope Gateway. Support for the exhibition has been provided by the Scottish Arts Council. The story of some of the pieces is told in this book and also on a film produced by Circa Media. In tandem with the crafts project the Royal Botanic Garden Edinburgh has run a number of community projects with the support of Scottish Natural Heritage. These have involved both children and adults from communities in Edinburgh, Midlothian and Fife. Craft workers, musicians, storytellers, poets and artists have been enlisted in a celebration of Scottish woodlands in general and the wych elm tree in particular. Through the media of the arts, science and technology, dozens of people, of all ages, have developed a personal and intimate appreciation of the wych elm in Scotland.

The Wych Elm Project is an excellent example of the kind of multidisciplinary project we will stage within the John Hope Gateway as we continue our exploration of whether there are boundaries to the creativity a botanic garden can express. If there are limits we have yet to discover them. By setting aside traditional distinctions between art and science we can foster an exciting and innovative approach to exploring Scottish culture and our shared natural heritage in a world that is changing faster than at any time in history.

Professor Stephen Blackmore FRSE
Regius Keeper
Royal Botanic Garden Edinburgh

Wych elm-dominated
woodland adjacent to the
River Helmsdale, Highland.
Image: RBGE/Max Coleman.

Foreword

The ravages of Dutch elm disease have made it all too easy to overlook the role of wych elm in the ecology of our ancient and semi-natural woodland. Bleached skeletons of elms are now a familiar sight in the countryside. Despite the abundance of timber created by disease there have been few commercial uses for elm in recent times. The wood can be difficult to work, but the beauty of the pattern and colour of the grain makes the reward worth the effort.

Over the past few years Forestry Commission Scotland has assisted in raising the profile of traditional uses of Scottish timber through organisations such as the Scottish Furniture Makers Association and the Association of Scottish Hardwood Sawmillers. It is, therefore, heartening in these days of globalised mass production to be able to celebrate the craftsmanship of professional men and women who are able to provide an alternative for the discerning customer.

We are also undertaking the Native Woodlands Survey of Scotland to survey and map all native woods in Scotland. The survey is collecting information on presence and canopy cover of all tree and shrub species in native woods (woods with mainly native species in the canopy), split into each of the various growth stages including regeneration, shrub layer, pole, mature and veteran trees. This will greatly improve our knowledge of the distribution and population structure of wych elm.

The Wych Elm Project has demonstrated how ordinary people can derive pleasure and satisfaction from working with wood and simply

being out in woodlands. The four community projects highlighted in this book enabled a variety of people of different ages and from all walks of life to learn new skills, share experiences and explore their own creativity. I am delighted that Forestry Commission Scotland was able to help in these projects and that the Wych Elm Project has provided further evidence of the benefits such involvement brings to individuals and communities.

Dr Bob McIntosh FICFor, FRICS
Director
Forestry Commission Scotland

Wych Elm

Flushes in spring, a pinkish haze.
The raindrop slows up on toothy leaves.

Cluster of fruit on a flat winged plate.
Duff or dent, the boards won't split.

Not for burning, curls of gold.
Even the very flames are cold.

Bends archer's bow, furrows its bark.
A bronze age burial in an elm trunk.

The ruined bole the beetle scores,
Borer of tunnels, bearer of killer spores.

The young sapling will resist disease,
Water-pipes bring music of the trees.

Valerie Gillies

Wych elm painting by Toby Gough.

A Highly Prized Tree

The Wych or Scotch Elm

By Max Coleman

A Highly Prized Tree

The Wych or Scotch Elm

By Max Coleman

Sir Thomas Dick Lauder edited a revised version of William Gilpin's *Remarks on Forest Scenery, and other Woodland Views* published in 1834. In it he wrote enthusiastically of the merits of the wych elm (*Ulmus glabra*):

> For our parts, we consider the wych, or Scottish elm, as one of the most beautiful trees in our British sylva. The trunk is so bold and picturesque in form, covered, as it frequently is, with huge excrescences; the limbs and branches are so free and graceful in their growth, and the foliage is so rich, without being heavy or clumpy as a whole, and the head is generally so finely massed, and yet so well broken, as to render it one of the noblest of park trees; and when it grows wildly amid the rocky scenery of its native Scotland, there is no tree which assumes so great or so pleasing a variety of character. Our associations with it in such scenes lead us to prize it highly.

Between 23rd and 25th June 2003 a majestic old wych elm that more than lived up to Lauder's eulogy was felled at the Royal Botanic Garden Edinburgh due to Dutch elm disease. A count of the growth rings revealed the tree was 197 years old. It may have been the oldest tree in the Garden and certainly predated the move of the Royal Botanic Garden Edinburgh from its former site off Leith Walk in 1820. The tree itself was massive. It was listed among the largest examples of its kind in *Alan Mitchell's Trees of Britain*, a compendium of outstanding specimen trees compiled by one of Britain's leading tree experts. The crown was very broad and quite symmetrical. It had the look of a tree that had never been restricted by neighbours, a classic open-grown specimen completely unlike a narrow woodland tree. The tree was a dominant presence, and its felling left a gaping hole.

Almost as soon as the trunk hit the ground plans were being made to use the wood for an exhibition of contemporary Scottish furniture and craft to celebrate the tree and let it live on in many new forms. At an early stage in what became the Wych Elm Project it was decided to write a book that could record the finished work, its process of creation and the wider story of wych elm with a Scottish slant. (Being at home where lowland meets upland the wych elm is generally more abundant in Scotland than in England.) A book covering the history, folklore, uses, associated wildlife and current status, in light of the ongoing Dutch elm disease epidemic, seemed to be a glaring omission in the literature.

Exhibitions based around the wood of a single tree have featured at the Royal Botanic Garden Edinburgh twice before. In 1993 *The Botanic Ash* used an ash tree from the Garden, and in 2001 *One Tree* used a pedunculate

oak from Tatton Park in Cheshire. Oak, ash and elm are the three large native Scottish broadleaved trees, making the Wych Elm Project the obvious completion of a trilogy.

Elms are etched in the British psyche for their sudden disappearance due to Dutch elm disease in the 1970s. Anyone who can remember that decade is likely to remember the demise of the elm. The story of how the fungus responsible evolved from a mild to a virulent pathogen and spread via the international trade in timber is told in Chapter 7. The disease had such a devastating impact on the British landscape that even people who didn't have much interest in trees or the environment took notice. My local park in London lost its many towering elms. I would have been only four or five years old at the time – too young to really appreciate that there were different types of tree – but I remember the disappearance of the elms. First there were the tell-tale signs of yellowing foliage. Then, as if spirited away in the night, the trees vanished to leave huge stumps ideal for a small boy to climb on. Eventually the roots were dug out, the pits filled in, and new turf laid. All trace of the trees had been erased.

During the mid 1970s the bleached skeletal forms of dead elms provided the backdrop to a journey through the countryside. The scale of the loss was quite staggering. By the 1990s Forestry Commission estimates put the number of elms lost at over 25 million, and it is hard to

Above: The Garden's wych elm shortly after felling. Diseased elms have their bark removed to prevent them from becoming breeding sites for the beetles that spread Dutch elm disease. Image: RBGE/Debbie White.

Left: The wych elm being felled by the arboriculture team at the Royal Botanic Garden Edinburgh. Image: RBGE/Debbie White.

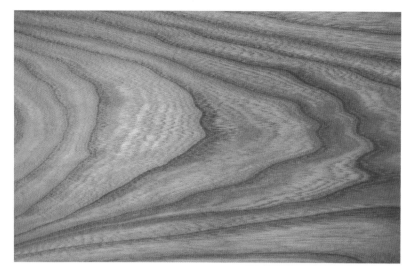

Above: The grain of wych elm displays decorative patterns known as 'partridge breast' which results from the interweaving of the wood fibres. Image: RBGE/Robert Unwin.

believe now that elms were once a dominant feature of the landscape in many areas. It has become clear with the passage of time that Dutch elm disease has been the worst British tree disease epidemic in living memory.

At the height of the epidemic there was outcry for action, but no realistic solutions were found and the disease ran its course in all but a few areas where careful sanitation measures were enforced. As a result, the elm has become something of a forgotten tree.

Scotland has been a stronghold of the wych elm for millennia. Everyone thinks of Scots pine (*Pinus sylvestris*) when they think of trees in Scotland, but in many ways the wych elm should be just as much an iconic Scottish tree. It has been growing in Scotland for around 9,000 years and its natural distribution in Scotland is actually far wider than that of the pine. Despite occurring patchily, wych elm is found throughout Scotland with the exception of the peatlands and high ground above about 500 m.

The Wych Elm Project has drawn together 22 makers, mainly living in Scotland, who have undertaken a wide variety of commissions using the wood of the Royal Botanic Garden Edinburgh's wych elm (see Chapter 10). An integral part of the project has been to document the process of dialogue that takes place between the maker and commissioner that ultimately results in a finished piece of work. To bring some of the pieces, and the people behind them, to life the Wych Elm Project

has been documented in film. The inspiration behind a piece and the practicalities of making it a reality come across on film. We are given a glimpse into the creative process.

Elm is an extremely useful wood. It ranks among the best native hardwoods and has some distinctive qualities that suit it to some uses and not others. The wood gains many of its characteristics from the grain structure. In elm wood the individual wood fibres interweave to produce cross-grained wood. This interweaving gives the wood great structural strength and resistance to splitting and has resulted in some traditional uses where such qualities were essential. The hubs of wooden wheels and the keels of wooden ships are two examples where the strength of elm wood is relied upon at the points of highest stress. Another characteristic of elm is its ability to resist rotting when in constant contact with water. As a result certain parts of waterwheels and the first water pipes were made of elm. But elm is extremely versatile and the list of traditional uses is correspondingly long, even extending to the use of its nutritious foliage as animal fodder. Chapter 4 reviews the past and present uses of elm and the growth in interest among furniture designers and makers.

Dutch elm disease has resulted in large amounts of wych elm being available to those who make things from wood. This abundance of wych elm has even influenced individual makers' styles. The most obvious example of this is the work of the late Tim Stead with its organic forms and convoluted edges. In Stead's work the burrs (large lumpy outgrowths on trunks and branches), rather than being cut off, are incorporated and become central to the piece. By slicing through burrs Stead reveals the extraordinary patterns of the grain within.

Early in the process of researching wych elm folklore it was realised there might be insufficient material for a chapter on the subject. Folklore, by its very nature, is rarely written down so there is a tendency for it to get lost over time. However, beliefs in one area often have equivalents in other areas so Chapter 3, which covers folklore, has widened its scope to include all elms. Although the folklore and cultural associations of elm in general have been thoroughly explored in Dick Richens' seminal book *Elm*, the significance of wych elm to the Scots has never been adequately documented.

A Gaelic cultural association with wych elm is seen in its use in the Ogham Tree Alphabet. Although never in widespread use, the Ogham alphabet was a device used by Gaelic scholars from the late Iron Age to the early Middle Ages in which trees were used to represent each letter of the alphabet. Wych elm, *ailm* in Old Gaelic or *leamhan* in Modern Scots Gaelic, represents A, the 14th letter of the Ogham alphabet.

By bringing together material on the lore, cultural associations and past uses of elm this book highlights the importance of the elm tree to people through the ages. It is well established that elms have been culturally important to many peoples. As a result of the research involved in this book we know a little more about what wych elms meant to the Scots. For instance, the use of wych elm for arrow manufacture on the island of Mull probably says as much about Highland ingenuity and a culture of 'making do' as it does about the suitability of elm for arrows.

Wych elms support a wide variety of associated wildlife. Chief amongst this in a Scottish context are lichens and fungi (see Chapters 5 and 6). Lichens are an intimate and mutually beneficial association of a fungus with an algal partner. The fungus provides shelter for the alga which in return provides the fungus with food in the form of sugars produced by photosynthesis. For this reason lichens need light to live and can be seen growing on various surfaces including the trunks and branches of trees. Lichens are visible throughout the year as colourful crusts and variously tufted or leafy outgrowths on elm bark. The fungus-alga partnership is not parasitic on the tree and does it no harm. Some lichens are even potentially beneficial as they fix nitrogen from the air which is then washed into the soil where it acts as fertiliser.

Fungi are much more seasonal and are often hidden away underground in the roots or in the

Wych elm near Carlops, Scottish Borders.
Image: RBGE/Max Coleman.

dead or living tissue as fine filamentous threads called mycelium. Here they grow and wait for the right conditions to produce fruiting bodies, the familiar caps on stalks, brackets and a variety of other structures that disperse the spores to start the next generation. Those that associate with living roots, mycorrhizae, help them to extract minerals from the soil in return for food and shelter from the tree.

Although no lichens or fungi are entirely restricted to wych elm there are some that show a very strong association and a larger number that, despite often occurring on other species of tree, do rely to some extent on elms for their survival.

The reason that certain fungi and lichens associate with wych elm is because the bark or wood or some characteristic of the living tissue provides just the right conditions for growth. The chemical composition, acidity/alkalinity or various other factors will in some way be particularly suitable whilst other tree species tend to be less suitable. These associations may have evolved over very long periods of time. When the association is strong, and other species rarely provide what is needed, the fate of two organisms becomes inextricably linked. A good example of this from the insect world is the white-letter hairstreak, *Strymonidia w-album*. This species of butterfly uses elm as the larval foodplant. Without elms the caterpillars have nothing to eat and the species cannot survive. As a result, the white-letter hairstreak in Britain has undergone a decline that mirrors the decline of elm. This butterfly is restricted to England where it feeds on all elms but seems to have a preference for wych elm. A number of butterflies have recently extended their ranges north, possibly linked to climate change. Perhaps the white-letter hairstreak in Scotland will be something to look forward to in the future?

In a similar case Scotland has become the British headquarters of the orange-fruited elm-lichen, *Caloplaca luteoalba*. Prior to Dutch elm disease this lichen was fairly widespread in eastern Britain. However, its strong association with elm resulted in a decline, mirroring that of the elm, to the point where virtually all the remaining sites for this lichen are to be found in eastern Scotland.

The chemical composition of elm bark is associated with the development of a colourful

Above: The white-letter hairstreak, *Strymonidia w-album*, is completely reliant upon elm as its larval foodplant. Image: © Paul Kipling, www.ukbutterflies.co.uk

Right: The lichen *Physcia aipolia*. Image: Mike Sutcliffe.

community of lichens in yellows and greys known as the 'Xanthorion' community. Elm bark is not acidic like oak bark and is often enriched by dust deposition from surrounding agricultural operations. Wych elms in open conditions are where classic *Xanthorion* lichen communities are found. The importance of subtle differences in bark chemistry is turning out to be crucial for lichens. Research on aspen has recently shown that variation in bark chemistry between individuals of the same species can be seen in the composition of the lichen communities found growing on the trees.

It has been known since the 1960s, when fossil pollen was first widely used to reconstruct vegetation history, that wych elm had undergone a massive decline right across northwestern Europe around the end of the Atlantic climatic optimum about 5,800 years ago. This pattern has come to be known as the 'Elm Decline'. A consensus of opinion is that this decline was driven by both an earlier epidemic of disease and the impacts of early human agriculture in the form of tree clearance and the lopping of elm for animal fodder.

In the context of an earlier decline, from which there was evidently some recovery, we can begin to put the current epidemic into some sort of perspective. Elms have the potential to recover (see Chapter 8). Wych elms regenerate from the abundant seeds produced in most years, and apparently dead trees often sprout from the base. Most encouragingly some elms appear to remain healthy even when nearby trees are killed. Exactly how these trees survive is not yet clear. It is probably not the case that all of these trees are truly disease resistant. Such survivors have tended to die when artificially inoculated with the disease in disease-resistance trials. In nature the disease is transmitted from tree to tree by the feeding activity of tiny elm bark beetles. Beetles emerge from the trunk of a dead elm covered in the spores of the Dutch elm disease fungus. They then fly to other elms to feed on the bark of young twigs and in the process infect the trees with the disease. One plausible theory of what may be happening, and much more

work is needed here, is that the surviving trees are simply not producing the right cocktail of smells that allow elm bark beetles to locate elms.

Inoculation trials where elms are infected with Dutch elm disease under controlled conditions have shown that truly resistant individuals do exist, but that they are extremely rare.

Much of the effort to counter the effects of Dutch elm disease has revolved around selection and breeding programmes. European elms have been crossed with disease-resistant Asian species to produce disease-resistant cultivars. Some of these cultivars have also been derived from disease-resistant forms of the American

Above: The lichen *Xanthoria polycarpa*. Image: Mike Sutcliffe.

Above: The Garden's wych elm
photographed in early summer.
Image: RBGE archive.

elm, *Ulmus americana*. The product of this work in the USA, the Netherlands, France and Italy has been a range of cultivars with some degree of resistance. From a horticultural and urban tree planting perspective the results must be regarded as a success. The only problem is that the elms produced tend to look rather different to the British elms. This is particularly true in the case of the wych elm.

To complement the work on horticultural elms based on controlled crossing and selection we should also be exploring how some of our elms survive in the wider countryside unscathed. Is there a genetic basis to this? Are we simply seeing a dramatic example of natural selection? Is there some form of biological control that we do not fully understand? These questions and many more need to be answered.

This book is a celebration both of the wych elm in general and of a particular tree, explored through the fields of craft and woodworking. Drawing together a group of people who

could focus their different areas of expertise on the wych elm has produced a book of far greater depth than would have been possible with a single author. It is hoped the book will also help raise the profile of the wych elm and encourage efforts to conserve it.

The association between elms and people is strong and reaches back deep into prehistory. Roger Deakin eloquently touched on some of the best-known links in his book *Wildwood: A Journey Through Trees*:

> As with the elm hub of a cart wheel, or the elm keel of a wooden ship, it is the elm seat that holds together the chair. Elm always seems to be at the axis of things. When bells ring out from the church tower, they swing on massive timber stocks of elm.

We have relied on elms for millennia, but if elms are to reclaim their place in the British landscape in the foreseeable future they now rely on us.

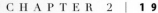

Wych elm overlooking the North Sea
near Berriedale, Highland.
Image: RBGE/Max Coleman.

Elm of the Brae
Natural History and Identification
By Max Coleman

Elm of the Brae
Natural History and Identification

By Max Coleman

Below: The hardiness of wych elm allows it to occupy highland locations as seen here in Glen Lochay near Loch Tay, Perthshire. Image: RBGE/Max Coleman.

The wych elm is very much a tree of the hills (braes in Scots) and increases in abundance in the hilly districts of the north and west of Britain. In 1791 William Gilpin gave a summary of the preferences of wych elm, in his *Remarks on Forest Scenery, and other Woodland Views*, that highlighted this association with hills:

> The wich-elm is a native of Scotland, where it is found not only in the plains, and vallies of the lowlands; but is hardy enough to climb the steeps, and flourish in the remotest highlands: tho it does not attain, in those climates, the size, which it attains in England.

The reasons why a plant species thrives in one area but is absent from another are many and complex. Factors such as chance do play a role. By chance a species may have dispersed to one area but not another and yet both are equally suited to its growth. In addition to the effects of chance a species might be expected to be found in the areas that provide the conditions it needs to grow and, most importantly, reproduce. Teasing out what these conditions are is the job of ecologists and plant physiologists. What soil type, rainfall and temperature does a species need? Is it frost hardy? What are the environmental limiting factors? But even

this is not the whole story of why a plant grows where it does.

For one thing environmental conditions are not stable for any great length of time and plants have moved around the planet in response to natural cycles of climate change. Past events influence present distribution. Various forms of fossil evidence allow us to reconstruct vegetation history and the movements of plants. Fossil pollen has been particularly useful as many of our trees (including elms) are wind pollinated and produce abundant pollen that is preserved in peat bogs and lake sediments.

Before delving into the details of the history and ecology of wych elm we need to first confront the thorny issue of elm identification. The naming of European elms has a history stretching back to the Greek philosopher Theophrastus, who wrote extensively on botany. The Renaissance herbalists of northern Europe attempted to equate the elms they were familiar with to the names assigned by the early Greek and Roman authors. This generally led to a good deal of confusion, and it was not until the publication of the second edition of Gerard's herbal in 1633 that four kinds of British elm were named that can be unambiguously identified today. At this time plants were often given phrase names, or polynomials, in the form of short descriptions in Latin. What is clearly the wych elm appears in Gerard's herbal as *Ulmus folio latissimo scabro*, with a vernacular name of 'witch hasell'. The idea of using shorter, more memorable names was promoted by Linnaeus in his *Species Plantarum* of 1753. In this book, which included all of the then known plant species, Linnaeus gave each species a two-part name called a 'binomial'. This system gradually found favour and eventually *Species Plantarum* was adopted as the starting point for modern plant taxonomy.

Linnaeus himself only recognised one species of elm in Europe, *Ulmus campestris*, but this name has been abandoned as ambiguous. The first British botanist to apply the binomial naming system to the elms was William Hudson in 1762. Hudson gave us the first binomial

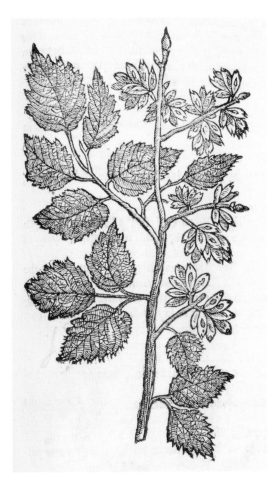

name for the wych elm – *Ulmus glabra* – which has priority over all later names. Unfortunately, Hudson's name was a poor choice as *glabra* refers to something being glabrous, meaning smooth, and the leaves of wych elm are roughly hairy. It is claimed the name refers to the smooth bark, but even the bark is only smooth in young trees. Overall Hudson's treatment of the British elms was as confused as much that had gone before.

The task of identifying elms has certainly not been helped by the proliferation of names with poor descriptions. However, the problem does in fact lie with a genuinely complex pattern of morphological variation. As a result, elms have acquired the reputation of being difficult to identify, even for the experienced botanist. The result is a classic case of disagreement between splitters, who like to recognise many subtly distinct species, and lumpers, who prefer to focus on similarities and accept fewer, but more variable, species.

Moss-covered trunk of wych elm near Carlops, Scottish Borders.
Image: RBGE/Max Coleman.

During the 20th century two very different interpretations of the British elms were proposed. Dick Richens recognised two species: the wych elm and a variable collection of forms that he grouped and called the field elm, *Ulmus minor*. He believed the field elm was an ancient introduction from continental Europe and that the variation in form reflected different parts of the wide geographical spread of the species. Early introduction from the Bronze Age onwards was argued for on the grounds of the great utility of elm and the possible cult status of elm in some Celtic cultures. In contrast, Ronald Melville at Kew recognised six species, some apparently unique to Britain, as well as complex hybrid combinations of these species. Not surprisingly, a lively disagreement on elm classification was conducted by Richens and Melville in the scientific literature.

The advent of DNA fingerprinting has shed considerable light on the question of how many elm species to recognise. A number of studies have now shown that distinctive forms that Melville elevated to species and Richens lumped together as field elm are single clones. What this means is that although the trees in question may occur across a wide area of Britain they are all genetically identical to each other and have been propagated by vegetative means such as cuttings or root suckers.

The field elms as a group are strongly suckering. They send up shoots from their roots that grow into new trees and by this means can spread a single clone over many metres. However, there is no evidence they could spread over the considerable ranges of some of the clones. Human intervention is the only reasonable conclusion. Sadly, this means that enigmatic British elms such as Plot's elm, *Ulmus plotii*, and English elm, *Ulmus procera*, have turned out to be single clones of field elm and are essentially prehistoric cultivated plants. Although Richens did not have DNA evidence to prove it, he got the story right by recognising a series of clones and grouping them together as a variable species. But Melville was also right to identify hybridisation as an important factor in the complex pattern of variation in the British elms. To summarise a complicated picture: Britain has two species of elm – suckering field elm that includes many distinctive forms, and non-suckering wych elm.

An unresolved argument is whether or not field elm is native in Britain. The difficulty with accepting field elm as native is that it does not, with a few possible exceptions, occur in recognisable associations or communities of native plants. It is generally a hedgerow tree and where it does occur in woodland it is an invader from hedgerows or former human habitation within the woodland. Field elm is a tree of central and southern Europe and if it was native it would have been limited to southern England. It has been suggested that field elm was a component of floodplain woodlands that were destroyed thousands of years ago by early agriculture. Unfortunately, pollen analysis cannot sort this problem out as the pollen of wych elm and field elm is indistinguishable. In Scotland this is all rather academic as there is no evidence here to suggest field elm is a native tree.

The introduction of a diverse range of field elm types to the British flora is not the sole reason why elm identification has become so controversial. Where different elm species come into contact there seem to be weak barriers to hybridisation. Flowering times are slightly offset between wych elm and field elm but despite this hybrids tend to arise between these species. They have probably been kept separate by ecological differences that have given rise to largely non-overlapping ranges. Where the ranges do overlap wych elm is found at higher altitudes than field elm. When humans brought field elms north into the range of wych elm hybridisation occurred and produced some of the aforementioned problems experienced with elm identification.

Many zoologists advocate what is called the 'biological species concept'. Here species are defined by barriers to reproduction. It could be argued that as there appear to be weak barriers to interbreeding between wych elm and field elm they constitute nothing more than subspecies or varieties of a single species.

Only the most dedicated of lumpers would advocate this approach today. The distinction of wych elm and field elm is clear despite the presence of hybrids in some areas. Among plants there are many examples of two species well defined by morphological differences blending together at points of contact to form what are called 'hybrid swarms'. This is the main reason why the biological species concept has not been popular with botanists.

Within Britain the natural variation seen within wych elm is not sufficiently marked or consistently distributed to allow the recognition

Above: A cultivar of wych elm called 'Nana' that forms a domed crown about three metres high. This specimen at the Royal Botanic Garden Edinburgh grows in the Rock Garden. Image: RBGE/Max Coleman.

Left: Camperdown elm, *Ulmus glabra* 'Camperdownii', is a weeping cultivar. This specimen in the cemetery of St Cuthbert's Church in Edinburgh is among the largest known. Image: RBGE/Max Coleman.

Right: Wych elm pollen
viewed with a scanning
electron microscope.
Image: RBGE/Frieda Christie.

Far right: Wych elm pollen
viewed with a compound
light microscope.
Image: RBGE/Frieda Christie.

Below: The flowers of
wych elm are an early herald
of spring during March.
Image: RBGE/Max Coleman.

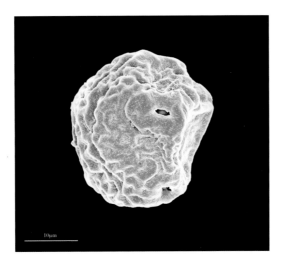

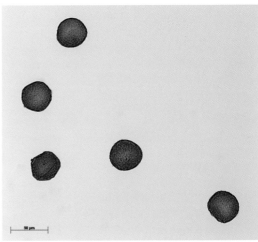

of subspecies or varieties. However, wych elm, like many trees, has produced spontaneous mutants that have in some cases become popular horticultural trees. Among the commonly encountered cultivars of wych elm are two pendulous forms that arose in Scotland. 'Camperdownii' has a contorted growth pattern and a very pendulous habit. It arose at Camperdown House near Dundee and the original tree still grows there. 'Horizontalis' has a more spreading, gently arched form and it arose in a batch of seedlings in a Perth nursery. Both forms are often seen planted in Victorian cemeteries. An erect-growing form, 'Exoniensis', with curiously curled leaves, arose near Exeter. York produced a distinctive golden-leaved wych elm called

'Lutescens' which is now uncommon. Very rarely a dwarf form called 'Nana' is seen that probably resulted from an infection known as a 'witch's broom' that stunts growth.

The British flora has had to retreat to southern Europe during periods of severe climate cooling, the so-called Ice Ages, and then spread north again as the climate warmed in the following interglacial. This ebb and flow of plants across Europe happened many times during the Quaternary period, roughly 1.8 million years ago to the present, and is the reason that Britain – and Scotland in particular – has a small flora with a restricted number of trees. Scotland's 14 to 21 native trees (the difference being due to how you define a tree) are those that have returned under their own steam in the current interglacial. They include the wych elm.

Pollen, the dust-like substance released by the male part of the plant, is produced in great abundance by wind-pollinated plants such as wych elm, and has been used to unravel the process of colonisation after the ice retreated and the climate warmed sufficiently to support tree growth. Pollen is readily preserved in certain deposits, such as lake sediments and peat, and can be identified with reasonable precision. The distinctive shape and surface architecture means that groups of related species and some individual species can be recognised. Combining this with radiocarbon dating, it is possible to travel back in time and reconstruct the vegetation growing in a particular area. This is done by

extracting cores from lake beds and peat bogs and then identifying and quantifying pollen from a series of points along the core. In some deposits it is possible to go back year by year with the annual accretion of peat or sediment.

From around 13,000 years ago a largely treeless landscape, scoured of its vegetation by the power of ice and melt-water, emerged as the climate warmed. Pollen analysis across Britain and Europe has revealed a consistent pattern of tree colonisation. Hardy trees with small wind-blown seeds, such as birch and Scots pine, were the first to colonise from about 11,000 years ago when the pace of warming increased. These pioneers were followed by trees with larger, animal-dispersed seeds such as hazel and oak. The wych elm was

comparatively quick to return as the pollen record shows that it was widespread and abundant in Scotland from about 9,000 years ago. From about this time wych elm was also a conspicuous component of deciduous woodland across northwestern Europe and this situation persisted through the climatic optimum of the Atlantic (*c.* 8,000 to 5,000 years ago) when the wildwood of pre-agricultural Britain reached its fullest development in conditions warmer than today.

One of the most striking discoveries to come out of the study of fossil pollen is what is called the 'Elm Decline'. This event has been consistently dated to around 5,800 years ago from many sites across Europe. It is the sudden, widespread, and almost simultaneous

Above: Woodland containing wych elm at Latheronwheel north of Dunbeath, Highland. Image: RBGE/Max Coleman.

nature of the decline in elm pollen that is so remarkable and has led to so much speculation. Typically elm pollen is reduced by half and either stays at that level or recovers slowly. Human activity is often pointed to as the cause of the Elm Decline. The appearance of agriculture in Scotland around 6,000 years ago does coincide quite closely with the Elm Decline. Early farmers would have cleared the most fertile land for their crops and would have needed fodder for their livestock, and convincing links between elm and these two activities have been established. Elm occurs on the better soils, so it may have been selectively cleared. It is also the case that elm foliage is a nutritious fodder for animals, second only to ash for this purpose. The cyclical cutting of wych elm to produce animal fodder is a practice that has persisted in Norway to the present day. This type of management would effectively prevent pollen production.

It does seem very likely that human activity played a part in the Elm Decline. The principal objection to this has been that human influence

Above: Pollarding of wych elm for animal fodder has survived in Norway to the present and may once have occurred in Scotland. Image: Helen Read.

Right: Autumnal colour in wych elm often includes vivid yellows. Image: RBGE/Max Coleman.

would not have been sufficiently widespread to account for such a sudden decline across the whole of northwestern Europe. The other convincing theory advanced to explain the Elm Decline is that earlier waves of Dutch elm disease caused the elm population to collapse suddenly across a wide area. Fossil finds of one of the elm bark beetles responsible for spreading the fungal pathogen go back far enough to make the disease theory possible. In addition, sub-fossil elm wood from the time of the decline has recently been shown to have modifications in form that are typical of Dutch elm disease infection. Ample demonstration of the potential impact of disease is provided by the rapid demise of elms in Britain due to the current virulent strain of Dutch elm disease (see Chapters 1 and 7). Rather than viewing these theories as competing explanations there is a general consensus that they may well have acted in combination to bring about the Elm Decline.

Wych elm grows throughout most of Scotland, with the exception of the higher upland areas and waterlogged peatlands. It is not just widespread but common in many areas. This general abundance has given rise to the name 'Scotch elm'. Prior to Dutch elm disease

the wych elm was an important part of the landscape in many lowland and highland areas. Wind-blown seed and the ability to thrive in cool conditions both aided rapid colonisation of suitable areas. Although wych elm is widespread throughout Britain, it becomes more common in the north and west and is found growing up to a maximum altitude of about 530 m. In Scandinavia populations extend inside the Arctic Circle to about 67 °N. The predominantly northern European distribution extends into southern Europe with outliers on higher ground such as the Pyrenees, Alps, Carpathians and northern Balkan mountains.

The soils on which wych elm grows are moist and relatively fertile and are often derived from calcareous bedrock. Wych elm is also seen growing on crags and in ravine woodland.

There is an association between wych elm and both ash and lime (the latter in England only). Typically wych elm grows as a component of mixed deciduous woodland and wych elm-dominated woodlands are rare. For this reason the *National Vegetation Classification* does not recognise elmwoods as a type of woodland, although wych elm is recorded as being found in five distinct woodland communities recognised in the classification.

Woodland ecologist and historian Oliver Rackham recognises two elmwood types from eastern England, characterised by either field elms, which he calls suckering elms, or his lineage elms which may be hybrids between field elm and wych elm. In upland Britain he recognises small patches of elmwood where wych elm grows among other types of

Below: Elm fruits develop before the leaves emerge in spring. Image: RBGE/Max Coleman.

woodland. Rackham describes a woodland sequence, known as the highland-zone catena, from steep valley-sides on relatively infertile rock in the uplands. Here the upper and middle slopes are oakwood, while hazel occupies the lower part of the slope with a narrow fringe of wych elm at the bottom, and alder lining the stream. This pattern is interpreted as being the result of the leaching of minerals from the upper slopes and their accumulation at the base where the more nutrient-demanding trees take advantage of them.

George Peterken's woodland classification recognises four ash–wych elm stand types. Two of these, the calcareous ash–wych elm woods and the western valley ash–wych elm woods, occur in Scotland. Peterken also recognises two suckering elm stand types from England. The first, invasive elm woods, are the product of planted suckering field elms invading other woodland types. The second, valley elm woods, are an extremely rare type where field elms appear to be native and may represent a survival of the proposed natural floodplain habitat of the field elm in southern England.

The reproductive biology of wych elm marks it out as quite distinct from the field elm. Wych elm is generally a non-suckering elm, although it will coppice well and does often sprout from the base when the upper parts are killed by Dutch elm disease. For this reason the distribution of wych elm has not been reduced by Dutch elm disease, even if mature trees are now very rare in affected areas. However, the primary means of reproduction is seed. Wych elms produce bisexual flowers in the early spring and self-pollination is kept to a minimum through a combination of the pollen maturing and being shed prior to the female part being receptive and via self-sterility mechanisms that enable the plant to recognise its own pollen and prevent it from fertilising the ovules. Pollen moves between elms on the wind, potentially over considerable distances.

Field elm, in contrast, is strongly suckering and produces viable seed in Britain less consistently. It has been suggested that this is due to the species not being so well adapted to cold conditions during flowering. The English elm form of the field elm has long been known to display extreme sterility, even in southern Europe. Work is underway at the Royal Botanic Garden Edinburgh to explore why English elm is sterile. It has already been established that the embryo aborts at an early stage and one possibility is some form of chromosome imbalance which prevents normal development.

The wych elm population of Scotland is still in the throes of the Dutch elm disease epidemic that started on the south coast of England in the late 1960s. The disease arrived in Scotland in 1976 and has severely depleted the elms of southern Scotland. Although no national survey of the disease has been conducted, the main areas of impact are known to be the Scottish Borders, the Central Belt, the east coast south of Inverness, Perthshire and areas along the Great Glen. However, there are areas in the southwest, north and west and some islands that remain free of Dutch elm disease. It can only be hoped that natural barriers in the form of mountains and water continue to protect the surviving populations.

Above: A multi-stemmed wych elm that has possibly been pollarded in the past at Scroggies Brae near Carlops, Scottish Borders. Image: RBGE/Max Coleman.

The Brahan Elm is the largest-girthed wych elm in the United Kingdom. It grows at Brahan Estate, Easter Ross. Image: Michael Brooks.

A Very Tantalising Tree
Elm Lore and Associations

By Mary Beith

A Very Tantalising Tree

Elm Lore and Associations

By Mary Beith

Elm wood burns like churchyard mould
Even the very flames are cold.

So run two lines in a variation on the old lore for choosing logs to burn. Yet, in the space of a few days, two men, both with woodland experience, gave this writer opposing opinions on the effects of an elmwood fire. The first, perhaps because of an attachment to – and, years ago, much climbing of – a 19 m tall wych elm in the garden of his boyhood home in Anglesey, was very pleased with the logs which, he said, heated his house quite adequately all winter and he was happy enough with the slow burning. The second man was more in tune with age-old views on burning elm – not for him the dull fire giving off little heat. Yet both had used the logs in wood-burning stoves. How much is this a matter of expectations and requirements or, indeed, happy childhood memories that recall the words of John Keats?:

A laughing schoolboy, without grief or care,
Riding the springy branches of an elm.

In Scottish folklore, you would expect to find many stories about the wych elm and its uses in traditional medicine. It is, after all, a native tree with a lineage going back many millennia. However, where its wood is hard and heavy, its associations in Scottish legend and lore seem light and slippery. It makes tantalisingly brief, but all the same significant, appearances here and there, as in the story of the Barons of Bachuill, a tale retold by the collector of Gaelic traditions, Alexander Carmichael.

As Sir Donald Campbell of Airds, the villain of the piece (described by Carmichael as "steeped to his neck in fraud and guile"), lies dying he sends a messenger to bring him the good Baron of Bachuill whose lands he has stolen. But Campbell's wife, probably fearing that a repentant Sir Donald will return the lands – her inheritance – to the baron, sends a swifter messenger to intercept the first and order him to turn round for home immediately. All night long – and his death is terrible – Sir Donald keeps calling for the baron; and his wily wife carries on assuring him the baron would soon arrive.

> And all night long the black raven kept croaking in the elm tree above Black Sir Donald, as did the raven in the tree above the bed of Duncan. Before morning dawned, on a night of terrific wind and thunder and lightning, Black Sir Donald Campbell of Airds was dead.

The tree is specified as an elm when it need not have been. There is no other mention of it in the story, but in the old days people who told the story and those who listened to it would have understood the significance. Elms had a strong association with death, as did the raven with omens.

Here again, though, our perception of the elm is ambivalent, for it also had links in Gaelic lore with restoration to good health, and, while coffins are often made of elm, cradles were occasionally fashioned from it too. Highland archers had bows made of elm and on the island of Mull some people remember that the three wych elms at Brahadail, below Ben Mòr, provided materials for bows, and possibly arrows, made by generations of the Fletcher family for the Maclean warriors and hunters. The Fletchers' former houses are now very old ruins near the trees.

As the tree spreads its roots below ground and its branches into the air, so do the traditions associated with the elm go deep into time and far around the world. Its traditional lore and remedies will be explored more fully later in this chapter, but first, let us look at its inclusion in the Ogham alphabet of the early Gaels, in particular the scholars and similarly learned people.

The ancient Tree Alphabet, the *Ogham Chraobh*, may have come to Scotland from Ireland some 1,500 years ago when the Picts adopted Ogham inscriptions. Scholars in the Middle Ages revived for a time this alphabet, in which all the letters are the names of trees or shrubs. Several aspects of the alphabet and its origins remain a puzzle, but the mystery is part of its charm. Sometimes it is known as Beth-Luis-Nuin (or Nion) after the first three 'tree-letters', respectively birch, rowan and ash in English. The five vowels come at the very

Above: A rare representation of a medieval Scottish archer (left figure), in a detail of a hunting scene from the tomb of Alexander Macleod, St Clement's Church, Rodel, Harris. Image: Crown copyright: Royal Commission on the Ancient and Historical Monuments of Scotland.

end. Wych elm, in the more standard 18-letter alphabet (the number of letters can vary according to the period and place in which it was used), comes in at number 14, A for *ailm*. And this is where another question mark hangs over our slippery customer. The word *ailm* was anciently applied to the pine tree, but later came to mean an elm. The most common Gaelic word for a wych elm these days is *leamhan*, but in some cases this has been used for the lime. Another, far less common, Gaelic word for elm is *tuilm*, but this is also given to some oaks, in particular the holm oak (*Quercus ilex*). An interesting coincidence is that biblical scholars down the ages have had problems in tackling a Hebrew word for a certain tree in Isaiah 41:19 and 60:13 which has variously been translated as 'elm', 'pine' or 'oak'.

Old Irish tree lists, dating back to the 8th century, put trees into four categories: nobles, commoners or tenants, the lower orders and shrubs. Under the Irish Brehon Law, there was a sliding scale of punishments for illegal felling, according to the 'status' of the tree; thus elms, being 'commoners', attracted a lesser fine than the felling of oaks, which were among the 'nobles of the wood'.

Perhaps there is an echo of this practice, albeit with the elm being upgraded to the noble ranks of oak and ash, in this Scots rhyme:

The aik, the esh, the elm tree,
The Laird can hang for a' three;
But fir, saugh an' bitter weed,
The Laird may flyte an' make naething b'eet.

Here, the theft of the superior timber is a hanging offence, while the pilfering of pine (demoted from the old list of nobles), willow and elder merely merits a fierce telling-off.

Elms were sometimes planted in the Borders to ward off witchcraft. Perhaps 'wych' (pliable) was confused with 'witch', but there was a tradition that the magically inclined shunned the tree. Is there, one wonders, a connection between such beliefs and the fact that wych elm wands are much touted on internet sites as ideal tools of the trade for magicians?

As an educated literary man, the poet Tennyson might have been expected to know better. However, in *In Memoriam* we find the lines:

Witch-elms that counterchange the floor
Of this flat lawn with dusk and bright.

But Tennyson on elms will always be best recalled by his famous couplet from *The Princess*:

The moan of doves in immemorial elms
And murmuring of innumerable bees.

Sir Walter Scott does no better with his spelling at the beginning of *The Lady of the Lake*:

Harp of the North!
That mouldering long hast hung
On the witch-elm that shades
Saint Fillan's spring.

Trees, elms among them, often formed part of the Celtic bardic allegory of symbols and metaphors. A fine late example which crosses over into our modern perception of the qualities of trees occurs in a beautiful elegy to Alasdair of Glengarry, by the 17th-century Highland poet Sìleas na Ceapaich:

Bu tu 'n t-iubhar thar gach coillidh,
Bu tu 'n darach daingean làidir,
Bu tu 'n cuileann 's bu tu 'n draigheann,
Bu tu 'n t-abhall molach, blàthmhor,
Cha robh do dhàimh ris a' chritheann
Na do dhligheadh ris an fheàrna,

Cha robh bheag ionnad de
'n leamhan;
Bu tu leannan nam ban àlainn.
(You were the yew above every wood,
You were the strong steadfast oak,
You were the holly and the blackthorn,
You were the rough-barked, flower-laden
apple-tree,
You had no affinity with the aspen,
You were not obliged to the alder
You had nothing of the elm
[or lime] in you;
You were beloved of beautiful women.)

Some Gaelic scholars have argued that the tree in the penultimate line should be translated as lime rather than elm, but, going by her other knowing allusions to the actual and poetic personalities and attributes of trees, Sileas is surely far more likely to be saying that Alasdair had none of the bitter slipperiness of the elm, rather than that he had none of the gently revitalising aspects of the lime.

As mentioned, elms do not feature much in Scottish folklore. They make only rare appearances, mostly as items in a list. In Alexander Carmichael's splendid collection, the *Carmina Gadelica*, we find:

> *Tagh seilach nan allt, tagh calltain nan creag,*
> *tagh feàrna nan lòn, tagh beithe nan eas, tagh*
> *uinnseann na dubhair, tagh iubhar na leuma,*
> *tagh leamhan a bruthaich, tagh duire na grèine.*
> (Choose willow of the burn, choose hazel
> of the rock, choose alder of the bog, choose
> birch of the waterfall, choose ash of the shade,
> choose yew of the resilience, choose elm of
> the braes, choose oak of the sun.)

Alexander Nicolson's variation in his edition of Gaelic proverbs gives the trees as:

> *Seilach allt, calltainn chreag, feàrna bhog,*
> *beithe lag, uinnseann an deisear.*
> (Willow of the brook, hazel of the rock,
> alder of the bog, birch of the hollow,
> ash of the sunny slope.)

Above: Wych elm near Cowdenburn, Scottish Borders.
Image: Michael Brooks.

Above: Plate 11, *The Idle 'Prentice Executed at Tyburn* from Hogarth's *Industry and Idleness* series of 1747, showing the execution of the 'bad' apprentice, Tom Idle, at Tyburn, London. By the 18th century Tyburn was long established as a site of execution by hanging; it was called 'The Elms' as far back as the 14th century allegedly due to a prominent group of the trees that grew there. Image from *The Works of William Hogarth*, Thomas Clerk, 1812. London: R. Scholey.

As an alternative, Nicolson gives: *beithe a' chnuic*, birch of the knoll.

Given that alder, willow and elm do not make good firewood, this cannot be a memory-rhyme for gathering logs for the hearth – and science often confirms such practical tradition. It has been suggested that it relates to a Highland tradition of nine sacred woods that kindled the druidical fires at Beltane and Hallowe'en.

In wider British lore, the elm is featured in the *Cad Goddeu*, a 6th-century Welsh poem attributed to the bard Taliesin, where it is depicted as steadfast and unyielding in battle, qualities no doubt influenced by the actual durability and hardness of its timber. A number of Welsh poems of this period are believed to have had a strong Pictish influence, if not origin, resulting from a migration into Wales of Pictish tribes displaced by both Anglian (in the southeast) and Gaelic (in the west) settlers. There are good reasons,

for example, for accepting that the basis for the story of Tristan and Iseult may be Pictish in origin.

One of the earliest associations of elms and death (unless it is a much later addition to the original Greek legend) is the story that, as Orpheus mourned the loss of his beloved Eurydice, an elm grove sprang up at the sound of his music.

Dick Richens gives a wealth of cultural and traditional links for the tree, mainly from outwith Scotland, in his meticulously researched book, *Elm*, and inevitably there is much mention of the poor tree's supposed links with the valley of shadows. Never mind people in Scotland and Ireland being punished for stealing elm timber; in many places on the Continent, he tells us, courts were held under elm trees and a "large gallows elm existed until recently [1983] in the heart of Oporto in Portugal". England, too, had its share of elm gallows, such as the Gibbet Tree on London's Hampstead Heath. In Scotland, ash was the preferred tree for hanging, or for attaching the jougs (an iron collar or yoke) for minor offences. Richard Le Strange's *A History of Herbal Plants* offers what may be an ancient clue to all these connections between elms and punishment. He says that the Latin name for the tree, *ulmus*, now the generic name, "appears to refer to an ancient instrument of chastisement".

Commemorative elms did not fare much better in their associations. Richens remarks that they were frequently planted and dedicated to such acts as "shooting a deer, directing a battle, ordering someone to be hung or beheaded, or being hung or beheaded oneself". We must assume the last dedication was carried out prior to execution, or pause to wonder at the attraction of elm wands for magicians.

Then again, English elms were not necessarily regarded as mere passive participants in death and sorrow. It was commonly believed that the trees waited to drop a branch without warning so as to kill a man. Richard Jefferies was one writer who had a sardonic take on this superstition:

Elms are so patient, they will wait sixty or seventy years to do somebody an injury.

Rudyard Kipling was another:

Ellum she hateth mankind, and waiteth
Till every gust be laid,
To drop a limb on the head of him
That anyway trusts her shade.

So far as this writer is aware, Scottish wych elms have not invited any such reproach. Geoffrey Grigson, the poet, and author of *The Englishman's Flora* (a misleading title, since it also covers Scottish, Welsh and Irish plant-names and folklore), is fairness itself when he describes the wych elm as "A pretty tree, with more character or personality than the English Elm".

A more generous side to the human narrative imposed on the elm is the tree's close connection with vines. Opposed to what has been dubbed the 'Stygian Elm', with its gloom and doom, there is the 'Paradisiac Elm'. As Richens says, it is a "figure of the Golden Age of Paradise and Love", and it often features in the symbolism of the vine and elm. This perspective on the tree arose from the (mainly Italian) custom of training vines on elms, and the practice inspired poets from classical times onwards.

This 'marrying' vines to elms, so that the former did not rot on the ground, but clambered over the tree or its stump to produce healthy grapes, came to symbolise love and friendship and their triumph over death.

Anyone interested in a neat way to end a relationship or forestall an unwanted one that shows every chance of being, say, disagreeably clingy, might take a tip from the French: "*Attendez-moi sous l'orme*", they may murmur. "Meet me under the elm". And the person to whom this is said should understand that the tryst is not expected to take place. Justice conducted under a village elm had a reputation for, as Richens puts it, "inefficiency and procrastination".

The poet John Clare captured some of the happiest aspects of elms. There was one he would lie beneath and hear "the laugh of summer leaves above". Of another tree he wrote:

Below: The spread of a barren elm clone called the Atinian elm was promoted by the Romans who used it as a living framework for vine cultivation. Recent genetic research indicates that what is known in Britain as English elm (formerly *Ulmus procera*) is this ancient clone. The evidence supports spread from Italy to Spain and then from Spain to Britain. Image: RBGE/Max Coleman.

Old elm, that murmured in our chimney-top
The sweetest anthem autumn ever made.

And the great Milton, too:

I myself call to witness the groves,
streams and beloved village elms under
which, last summer – if I may speak of
the secrets of the goddesses – I recall
with delight that I received the highest
favour of the Muses.

While the Saint Fillan's spring mentioned above
in the quotation from *The Lady of the Lake*
would have been the one in Strathfillan in west
Perthshire, special healing rites used to be carried
out on St Fillan's Day at Millmore near Killin in
Stirlingshire. It was believed that the ritual of
washing in a waterfall and rubbing the wet skin
with a stone representing the afflicted part of
the body had a more potent influence when
carried out in the shade of an ancient elm.
If such 'cures' were effective, they would have
relied on a blend of belief in magic and the
intricacies of psychology. Perhaps we must take
account of the fact that, if a number of ailments
are stress-induced, it may be equally true that many
successful treatments are due to encouraging a
sense of quiet confidence and ease of mind.
In the case of the open-air washing under a
waterfall at Millmore, this may be stretching a
point – St Fillan's Day occurs in January.

More recently, a badly scalded one-year-old girl in the Lochalsh area of the West Highlands was treated in 1976 for the burns by a neighbour who applied the juice obtained from boiling the inner skin of elm bark. Despite the attentions of two doctors in the local surgery and the district nurses, standard medical methods had achieved little. One of the GPs remembers that the "neighbour had much success with the elm bark juice". A woman in Glenshiel, who was well known to the same doctor, also had a wound which, he said, "defied good orthodox treatment and which healed quickly after elm was applied".

Elm bark was, indeed, an authoritatively sanctioned treatment in a very comprehensive work on domestic medicine published in 1911. The writers – highly qualified medical men, unafraid of making the occasional acerbic remark – were happy, at a time when much professional scorn was poured on folk beliefs, to include this:

> ELM BARK, from the well-known tree, has been used as a remedy in skin diseases, especially in lepra and psoriasis; it is also slightly tonic and astringent. The decoction is made with two and a half ounces of the bark and a pint of distilled water, and the dose is from three to four fluid ounces.

Following that relatively modern and official advice, it is interesting that in AD 79 the Roman natural historian Pliny the Elder was also advocating the inner bark of elm for relieving leprous sores. He appears to have been quite a fan of the tree's medicinal properties (supposed or actual), claiming it would purge the bowels, get rid of phlegm, heal wounds and burns, bring brightness to the skin, make the looks more pleasing, and relieve swollen feet. One of the treatments on his list went far into the heart of the elm for its material:

> An application of the moisture too, that exudes [...] from the pith [medulla or core] of the tree when lopped, restores hair to the scalp and prevents it from falling out.

It was, perhaps, more an exercise in hope than efficacy. Then again, who knows? The American slippery elm, *Ulmus rubra*, is more closely related to the wych elm than to any other types of elm, and is still in use as an over-the-counter remedy for soothing digestive problems or for chesty coughs, as well as surviving the stringent demands of the modern American pharmacopoeia. In times past, and maybe this continues today, the native people of North America chewed on a piece of slippery elm inner bark for the same reasons, as well as having many

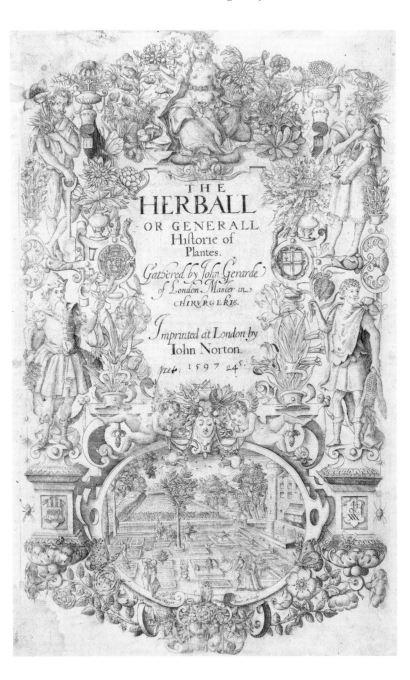

Below: Frontispiece from the first edition of Gerard's herbal of 1597. The lower part shows a scene in a physic garden. Gerard lists many medicinal and other uses of elm. Image: RBGE/Lynsey Wilson.

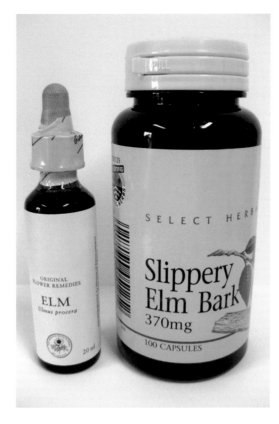

other medicinal uses for the tree. The slippery elm has a particularly high concentration of mucilaginous carbohydrate in the inner bark, but to some degree all species of elm have this 'slippery' substance in their bark.

In the Borders a familiar old name for the wych elm gives us another tease. In that region, the tree was known as 'chewbark', an undoubted reference to a probably forgotten custom of literally chewing on a piece of bark to soothe coughs and colds. Or it may have been because children in the eastern parts of the Borders would chew the inner bark of elm for the strange pleasure of its sticky moistness.

The medieval Welsh physicians of Myddfai, near Llandovery in Carmarthenshire, also employed the flowers and leaves of elms in their often complex-sounding remedies. For deafness they advised laying elm rods on the embers of a fire and collecting the juice that emerged in a clean pot. Then equal quantities of oil from a black eel, honey and betony juice were to be mixed into the elm sap and dropped into the ear which must then be plugged with the wool of a black lamb. This was deemed an 'effective cure'.

(And the deaf may add "If only...".) For a swelling or a skin inflammation, they took well-bruised inner elm bark and boiled it down to the thickness of honey. After sieving or straining it, they added barley meal and unsalted butter, and boiled the mixture into a poultice which was spread on flannel and applied to the afflicted area of skin. If a large amount of bark was used, it was said to heal small fractures. And here's one last example from their huge variety of treatments:

> For all kinds of heat and inflammation in the face, even if it were erysipelas: Take a quart of smithy water, a handful of the leaves of sage, a handful of the leaves of elm, or of the inner bark thereof, and a pennyworth of frankincense; boil these together to the half, and keep in an earthen vessel; anoint the face therewith.

Howards End, the novel by E.M. Forster, opens with a letter in which Helen Schlegel describes to her sister, Meg, the house that gives the book its title. The second paragraph describes the front garden and begins:

> Then there's a very big wych elm – to the left as you look up – leaning a little over the house, and standing on the boundary between the garden and the meadow. I quite love that tree already.

That tree exerts a strangely powerful presence throughout the book and all the complexities of its characters' developments. Even in the chapters where there is no mention of it, the reader can be curiously aware of that silent presence. Towards the end, Forster gives the wych elm an eerily beautiful voice:

> The present flowed by them like a stream. The tree rustled. It had made music before they were born, and would continue after their deaths, but its song was of the moment. The moment had passed. The tree rustled again. Their senses were sharpened, and they seemed to apprehend life. Life passed. The tree rustled again.

The Cornish pilot gig *Endurance* built by Andrew Nancarrow of Truro from Scottish wych elm. Image: Andrew Nancarrow.

Versatility and Utility
Uses of Elm Past and Present

By Ian Edwards

Versatility and Utility

Uses of Elm Past and Present

By Ian Edwards

Below: Portrait of Dr Nathaniel Spens, a prominent member of the Royal Company of Archers (the Sovereign's Bodyguard in Scotland), painted by Sir Henry Raeburn. Photographed from a private collection. Image: RBGE/Lynsey Wilson.

Wych elm, in common with all trees, has its particular idiosyncratic qualities, and two of these are indicated in two possible derivations of the name. As has been pointed out in Chapter 3, wych has nothing to do with witches. According to Geoffrey Grigson, author of *The Englishman's Flora*, it means 'switchy', from the Old English *wice* or *wic*, meaning pliant branch or timber. This corresponds with one frequently recorded use for the timber – supplying staves of strong, flexible wood for longbows.

An alternative derivation, quoted by C. Pierpont Johnson in another classic book, *The Useful Plants of Great Britain*, is from the word for salt-springs or *wyches* (as in Nantwych, Northwych and Droitwych). The brine tapped from the salt-springs was conveyed using troughs and pipes made from the wood of elm trees. This reflects another well-established property of elm timber – its ability to resist rot under conditions of permanent wetness.

The properties that make elm suitable for longbows are its elasticity and longitudinal toughness. Evidence for the use of elm longbows in Scotland has remained somewhat elusive. However, elsewhere in northern Europe elm seems to have been widely employed for this purpose, especially when the most favoured species, yew, was not available in the right dimensions.

Elm bows dating from the Mesolithic age have been found in Denmark, and in early Scandinavian literature the same word, *almr*, meant elm and bow. Elm longbows were also used by medieval Welsh archers and the names

of two Celtic tribes in prehistoric France reflect their preference in bow staves – the Eburovices (yew warriors) and the Lemovices (elm warriors). In England, during Edward IV's reign, an act was passed that required every Englishman, and Irishmen dwelling with Englishmen, to get a bow "either of yew, wych-hazel [wych elm], ashe [ash] or awburne [laburnum], or any other reasonable tree, according to their power".

In 1633, after the longbow had ceased to be a weapon of war, Thomas Johnson wrote about the use of elm for bows in the second edition of Gerard's herbal:

> Old men affirme, that when long
> boughes [bows] were in great use,
> there were very many made of the
> wood of this tree, for which purpose
> it is mentioned in the statutes of
> England by the name of witch hasell.

The Flodden campaign of 1513 included a force of 600 men armed with bows and halflangs (two-handed swords) under the command of Mac Gill'Eathain (Maclean) of Duart on Mull. The Macleans apparently commissioned their arrows from a local family, the Fletchers (from *Mac an fhleisdeir* meaning 'son of the arrow maker'), who are reputed to have used wych elm wood for the purpose. Many woods have been used for arrow making in the past and Maurice Thompson in *The Witchery of Archery* specifically mentions elm in relation to arrow making. Perhaps the Fletchers were using the straight young shoots from coppiced elm stools – unfortunately the details of arrow

Above left: Elm pipes from the City of Edinburgh Council collection showing how two pipes are joined. Image: RBGE/Max Coleman, with kind permission of the City of Edinburgh Council Museum Service.

This image: Elm pipes bringing seawater into the saltworks at St Monan's in Fife. Image: © Colin J. M. Martin. Licensor www.scran.ac.uk

making on Mull are probably lost in the mist of time.

Another link between wych elm and arrow making appears in the original edition of Gerard's herbal of 1597:

> The second kinde of Elme groweth likewise unto a great stature, with very hard and tough timber, whereof are made arrowes, wheeles, mill pullies and such other engines for the carriage of great waights [weights] and burthens [burdens].

The same qualities of strength combined with springiness that make elm suitable for bows also rendered the timber an appropriate choice for handles of ploughs, shafts of carts and other implements about the farm.

The use of hollowed out elm logs as water pipes was widespread and goes back to the 16th century. Logs of about 1.5 to 2.5 m in length were bored through. Originally this was done by hand, using an auger, but the process was later mechanised. One end of the log was tapered so it could be forced into the open end of the next log, with ample grease creating a snug and watertight fit. Pipes carrying spring water under pressure were sometimes deliberately bored latitudinally as well and the holes plugged with bungs. These could be removed if water was needed en route for dealing with fires – an early example of the fire hydrant system.

Edinburgh City Council Museums Collection Centre holds sections of the city's original elm water pipes, installed in 1685. These drew water from Comiston Spring to the head of the High Street. It is assumed that the wood for these pipes was of local origin and probably wych elm. Herbert Edlin in his 1949 classic *Woodland Crafts* makes the following observation, just as pertinent today in an age of plastic pipes, when we are being urged to source materials locally and reduce the impact of burning fossil fuels:

> If the boring of water pipes by hand strikes us as a laborious and uneconomic process, our present practice of digging up coal and iron ore, transporting them over great distances to blast furnaces and ironworks, and then carrying the finished pipes to their final resting places, would have appeared equally absurd to the old carpenters, who could produce pipes from trees growing on the spot.

There is evidence that in some parts of the British Isles elm trees were grown in a particular way to make the stem more suitable for the purpose of carrying water. The Earl of Haddington described how trees in the Thames valley had all their side branches cut "Bare as May poles", leaving just a small, bushy head, to create a knot-free, straight bole. Apparently the form of trees managed in this way was still discernible in the last century, long after the practice of cutting and boring pipes from trees had ceased. However, the fact that this description was by a Scotsman visiting England suggests that the custom may have been rare north of the border and may have been restricted to English field elms.

The ability to resist rot has also led to elm timber being used for waterwheels, flumes, piles and groynes. A recent example is the waterwheel at Livingston Mill in the Almond Valley Heritage Park, which was restored in the 1970s. Where the

wood is not immersed or saturated with water, for example in weather boarding, aerobic conditions can lead to decay and elm wood is not regarded as being especially durable without treatment. There are some contemporary examples of elm weather boarding in Scotland, mostly on outbuildings, for example on the Duke of Westminster's estate in northwest Sutherland and at Harestanes, in the Scottish Borders. The type of cladding is simple 'through and through' sawn boards with waney edges. The very wide boards are installed horizontally in a simple 'weatherboard' pattern with no attempt at profiling. To prolong its life estates will invariably treat elm cladding, creosote being the preservative of choice.

The association in literature and legend between elm and death goes back to Homer and beyond. Its place as guardian of the underworld in classical works became transformed to a kind of morbid observer of humans' allotted time-span by the time Rudyard Kipling wrote the lines "Ellum she hateth mankind, and waiteth"

(see Chapter 3). With such grim associations it is not surprising that elm wood was also chosen for coffin boards. However, if this symbolic connection with death was the main reason for selecting elm for coffins then its ability to resist rot must have been an important second. Much of the funeral business is dedicated to preserving the physical remains of the body for an extended period beyond burial and a watertight coffin must have slowed down the inevitable return to nature.

The use of elm in coffins seems to be very widely known; indeed it is the only traditional use that most people have ever heard of. However, very few people are buried in a solid elm coffin today and even in the days when coffins were made of solid wood, rather than laminate or veneered materials, the use of elm was far from universal. Oak rather than elm was often the wood of choice for the rich, and 'deal' (Scots pine) was the most widely used timber for the poor. According to two well-established Scottish coffin makers solid wood has recently made

Above: The hubs of cartwheels were traditionally made from elm. Here the holes are being drilled for the spokes.
Image: © Aberdeen City Council. Licensor www.scran.ac.uk

something of a comeback, with more orders coming in for solid oak caskets. However, elm is rarely used these days. Since Dutch elm disease good-quality timber has become harder to come by and because the wood moves it is not ideal for the modern, finely detailed designs. For those clients who want the rich colour and grain of elm wood there are elm-veneered coffins available with a variety of stains. In modern times when cremation is more popular than burial, at least in Britain, elm with its reputation as a poor firewood would seem less than ideal for coffins.

In the past, as today, when a farmer or crofter needed a piece of wood for a job he looked around his land for something that would best serve his need. It was a 'needs must' economy where utility was the prime driving force, especially where timber was scarce. A superb example is the medley of woods, some of it salvaged as driftwood that may have travelled from North America, to be found in an original Orkney chair. However, when a choice of woods is available the special properties of the individual timbers are appreciated.

The interweaving of the wood fibres that gives wych elm timber its elasticity also makes the wood very resistant to splitting. There are certain applications, when the wood is likely to undergo stress, where the cross-grained nature of the timber is especially valued. One of these is the hub of wooden wheels. The wheelwright would cut mortices into the hub into which the oak spokes were driven. According to one source, wych elm was the elm least likely to split. Another traditional use was the stocks on which large cast bells were hung (see Chapter 1). The same property came in useful where wood might be expected to get hard use – for example the boards on a cart (subject to frequent

shovelling), wheelbarrows, pulley blocks or the mould-boards on a plough. I have found elm makes an excellent chopping block, and *Flora Celtica* records a reference to unspecified 'engineering components' made from wych elm.

Wooden bowls were, and still are, frequently turned from elm. The patterned grain can make very attractive ornamental bowls but unpolished bowls have also served as kitchen and dining room utensils. The trick of producing a series of bowls, nesting inside each other like Russian dolls, often performed by a bodger with his pole-lathe, is rarely seen these days even though turners have far more sophisticated machinery.

This ability to accept knocks along with good rot-resistance makes elm a suitable timber for boat making, especially the keel that is for the most part submerged and gets the most abrasion. However, specific evidence of boats made from elm in Scotland is patchy. None of the prehistoric log boats excavated in Scotland were made from elm – the wood of choice was invariably oak. Contemporary wooden boat-builders also seem to prefer oak for the main structure of their craft, with European larch used for the planking. However, they do use elm for certain applications. Iain Oughtred, based on Skye, is an internationally renowned designer of small boats and in his prototypes he often uses elm for sections such as the transom.

Boats made entirely of elm seem to be more uncommon: the Cornish pilot gig is an exception. The rules of the Cornish Pilot Gig Association specify that to compete in races the boat should be made from Cornish narrow-leaved elm, a distinctive form of the field elm. Unfortunately with the advent of Dutch elm disease Cornish elm has become for all practical purposes extinct and the Association, which registers about six new boats a year, is now allowing other types of elm to be used. Some makers, including master boat-builder Andrew Nancarrow of Truro, have been given a dispensation to use wych elm timber for pilot gig construction. At least some of the supply has come from Lothian Trees and Timber, of Cousland, who cut and seasoned the timber for the Wych Elm Project.

When it is planed and polished the interwoven grain gives the timber an attractive decorative patterning known as partridge breast, or *pied d'chat* (cat's claw) in French. Wych elm wood also frequently has a greenish tinge or contains green streaks and these darker areas sometimes develop a greyish bloom, like the skin of a plum, even when the piece has been finished with oil. Mature woodland and hedgerow elms frequently produce burrs that give rise to the most distinctive and eccentric patterning in the wood.

Although today this rich variety of colouring and patterning typical of elm is seen as its most distinctive and (for some) attractive feature, this has not always been the case. In the past the grain was seen as 'too wild' for fine cabinet making and because it was also notoriously difficult to work, elm has had a lesser role than oak in traditional furniture. The important exception to this rule was the Windsor chair where elm was generally employed for the seat. Typically the legs and back of the Windsor were made of beech while the bowed back was steamed ash. The dished seat, however, was invariably cut from an elm board, hollowed out with an adze by a craftsman known as a bottomer.

Below left: An elm chair from a cottage near Leadhills, Lanarkshire. Image: © The Trustees of the National Museums of Scotland. Licensor www.scran.ac.uk

Below right: An elm chanter for highland bagpipes by McKay, London, from the early 19th century. Image: © The Trustees of the National Museums of Scotland. Licensor www.scran.ac.uk

Right: Tim Stead slicing
ash on the bandsaw.
Image: RBGE/Debbie White.

Below: Navigator Table
by Tim Stead in burr elm
stitched and inlaid.
Image: RBGE/Lynsey Wilson.

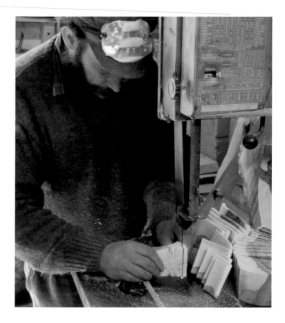

In more recent times elm has regained much more popularity as a furniture wood. The Berkshire family firm, Ercol, was a pioneer and their website gives a succinct summary of the company history:

> In 1920 a young designer called Lucian Ercolani started his own business in High Wycombe, the chairmaking capital of England. Here he perfected the technique of steam-bending wood in large quantities to form the famous Windsor Bow, and discovered how to 'tame' elm; a beautifully grained hardwood other furniture makers considered impossible to work with.

Ercol continue to use elm wood (English, European and American) as the seats of their contemporary chairs and for tables and sideboards. I grew up in a house with classic Ercol designs from the 1960s, and 40 years on the furniture has stood up to the wear and tear of family life remarkably well.

More recently, partly in the wake of Dutch elm disease creating an (albeit temporary) glut of mature timber often in large dimensions suitable for furniture making, there has been a huge interest among designers and furniture makers in using dead trees cut from hedgerows and parkland. Within Scotland, the resurgence in handcrafted furniture and the popularity of elm (largely wych elm) timber has been led by a group of designer-makers, of whom the best known

is the late Tim Stead. Much has already been written about Stead's iconic pieces and the Royal Botanic Garden Edinburgh has hosted three exhibitions of his work, including the recent, posthumous touring exhibition *With the Grain*.

Stead's genius, as the title of the exhibition and accompanying book suggests, was to exploit the natural character of the wood rather than hide it. Not only did he value the partridge breast grain in his work but he deliberately selected pieces that contained burrs, irregular outgrowths from the trunk of the tree, and incorporated the chaotic patterns and sculptured form into his work.

Most commentators have described Stead as being first and foremost a sculptor but it is his idiosyncratic furniture that he will be most remembered for. He was an anarchist-in-wood, not accepting the status quo of straight lines, uniform patterns and symmetry but revelling in the curves, scars, asymmetry and deformities so that each of his works was in fact an individual sculpture as well as a piece of functional furniture.

Stead's work has been hugely influential and imitators are so prolific that his widow Maggy Stead has jokingly referred to them as the 'inSteads'. However, the real legacy that has been gained from this radically different approach to woodworking is a new freedom of expression in which the character of the wood dictates the form. The fact that this design revolution

occurred in the Scottish Borders at the same time as Dutch elm disease decimated the majority of large wych elm trees in the region is probably no coincidence. The availability of very large, open-grown, mature elm trees, covered in burrs and pitted with holes, virtually free for the taking, provided the raw material for this explosion of creativity. Subsequently some contemporary makers, like Rob Elliot (see Chapter 10), have been able to make an ecological virtue out of using only dead elm trees in their work.

The value of wych elm to humans has been dominated by its importance as a timber but it has a variety of other uses. As mentioned, elm has a reputation as a poor firewood: "Elm logs like smouldering flax/No flame to be seen" and "Elmwood burns like churchyard mould/E'en the very flames are cold" are couplets from oft quoted firewood rhymes, yet this doesn't seem to have stopped many people using elm logs, often salvaged from dead trees, in their woodstoves (see Chapter 3). The recent increase in fuel prices, perhaps a foretaste of the fossil fuel crisis to come, along with a greater ecological conscience has spurred many people to invest in woodstoves for domestic heating or even cooking. This is bound to increase demand for seasoned hardwood logs and my experience is that if properly dried and mixed in with other hardwood species wych elm burns well enough in a good stove.

The Ainu indigenous people from northern Japan use the word *chikisani* for elm. This is derived from *chickisa* meaning fire-drilling, a primitive method of starting a fire from friction. Apparently elm is the wood they use preferentially for this purpose. Although it burns weakly, elm, being hard and dense, might be expected to retain the friction-generated heat well, although another type of material would be required as tinder for ignition. Undoubtedly fire-drilling was a common practice in Scotland in prehistoric times but whether elm was used in preference to other woods is unknown. This might provide the basis for an interesting practical research project at one of the Scottish centres now specialising in the reconstruction of prehistoric lifestyles.

The inner bark or bast of many trees can be used as cordage and the *Flora Celtica* database includes a single reference to the use of wych elm for rope making in Scotland, quoting Lightfoot's 18th-century *Flora Scotica*. The various websites devoted to 'bush-craft' indicate that modern-day primitives are still experimenting with cordage made from twisting, twining or plaiting the under-bark of elm.

A decoction or extract of the inner bark of elm could be found in the pharmacopoeias of most European cultures. There are a few tantalising references to the medicinal use of Scottish (presumably wych) elm bark. A contributor to the *Flora Celtica* project describes:

> ... a family remedy for diesel poisoning, using the mucosal substance from under the bark of wych elm, mixed with Solomon's seal [*Polygonatum multiflorum*]. Rubbed on as a salve, this mediaeval sounding unguent was said to successfully combat the sores produced from diesel having got under the skin.

As mentioned in Chapter 3, elm bark juice has also been used for burns and wounds.

Left: A copy of a Philip Clissett ladder-back chair by Tom Ball in ash with a woven seat from wych elm bark. Image: Tom Ball, www.tomschairs.com

Above: Wych elm leaves and fruits are edible when young and tender. Image: Forestry Commission Picture Library/ Isobel Cameron.

Below: The inner bark of elm was formerly used as cordage and is still used today for weaving and other traditional crafts. Image: Scott Blytt Jordens, www.dragonflycreations.co.uk

As the beneficial effects of wych elm extracts on burns have never been scientifically proven it is tempting to explain these cures in terms of psychosomatic assurances – the placebo effect. Dick Richens is one of the sceptics and states categorically: "Elms contain little of any physiologically active or medically useful substances". However, he does concede that the inner bark of the European species contains tannins that can be mildly astringent and the American species *Ulmus rubra*, known as the slippery elm, contains mucilaginous carbohydrates used to treat diarrhoea or dysentery. He later

says slippery elm is used for costive (constipated) patients. In her popular herbal Mrs Grieve does include the bark of the field elm as an antiscorbutic (preventing scurvy) but then goes on to give much more attention to the inner bark of the slippery elm as a demulcent, emollient, expectorant, diuretic and nutritive.

Today slippery elm bark is sold as a rather bland food supplement in health food shops. Perhaps in the past people in Britain ate the under-bark or leaves of native elms as they did in China during times of scarcity. A Baptist missionary, the Rev Timothy Richard, during the 1878 famine wrote:

> That people pull down their houses, sell their wives and daughters, eat roots and carrion, clay and leaves, is news nobody wonders at. It is the regular thing…
> The poorest people are dependent on willow and elm leaves, elm bark, and the various weeds… All the elm trees about many of the villages are stripped of their bark as high as the starving people can manage to get; they would peel them to the top but haven't the strength.

The Chinese are also recorded as eating elm flowers, dipped in flour and steamed, as well as the young fruits. Ray Mears, 'bush-craft specialist' and TV celebrity, makes no mention of the flowers but sings the praises of young elm fruits, eaten in spring, raw or cooked in soups. There seems to be further opportunity for some judicious experimentation by food for free enthusiasts.

Ray Mears also confirms that young wych elm leaves are edible although a bit rough when they first flush in May. Gerard's herbal of 1597 states that livestock were fed on elm leaves, so it is no surprise that an old Irish name for the wych elm was *cara ceathra*, meaning friend of cattle. The practice of feeding cattle with branches lopped off elm trees and dried for the winter still takes place in Scandinavia, but in Scotland, where we regard cows as grazing rather than browsing animals, the custom has long disappeared along with elm bows, rope and coffins.

Something to Sit On

Elm Lichens

By Brian Coppins

Use of a hand lens will reveal the form and colour of lichens in all their glory.
Image: RBGE/Max Coleman.

Something to Sit On

Elm Lichens

By Brian Coppins

Below: Elm gyalecta, *Gyalecta ulmi*, here growing on rock. Image: Nick Hodgetts.

Lichens are fungi living in a close association with algae, and this partnership allows them to grow on a wide range of surfaces, including rocks, trees and stabilised soil. When growing on trees, they have little if any physiological connection with the tree – this being in contrast to other fungi associated with trees. The lichen fungus obtains most of its nutrition from the algal partner, which produces carbohydrates by photosynthesis.

A lichen uses a tree for something to 'sit on', but individual lichens do have preferences or requirements for different conditions in terms of light or shade, wet and dry regimes, and acidity, nutrient status and texture of bark or wood. Different tree species offer a range of combinations of conditions. For example, mature beech trees have a dense canopy, creating much shade in summer, and a hard,

quickly drying bark. By contrast, mature ash trees have a much lighter canopy, and a rough, more water-retentive bark. For these reasons, although very few lichens are restricted to a given tree species, many are found more frequently on the one or two tree species that offer the lichen optimal conditions for establishment and growth.

In general, the trunk of mature elms has a rough bark with a low acidity, and a high water-holding capacity, and the canopy in summer is quite dense. However, these factors are subject to much variation depending on the situation and condition of the tree. In areas subject to acid rain the bark will be more acid, but in parkland and wayside situations influenced by wind-blown dust and animal excreta the bark will be more base-rich. Strongly basic bark can also be found on trunks below seeping wounds and alongside sap runs. Trees with a broken crown will have a less dense canopy and a better-lit trunk, although numerous epicormic branches on the trunk will cast a dense shade, even for trees in open habitats.

In Scotland, 267 species of lichen have been recorded from elm, representing about one sixth of all the 1,500 or so Scottish lichens. Very few of the 267 are confined to, or mainly found on, elm, although two rare priority species have 'elm' in their name, viz. elm gyalecta, *Gyalecta ulmi*, and orange-fruited elm-lichen, *Caloplaca luteoalba*. The former was known in the 1970s in the Glen Lyon woods on an elm, which has long since succumbed to Dutch elm disease, but was discovered in 2008 on an ancient elm near Inverfarigaig. Fortunately, this internationally

rare lichen is also known on calcareous rock outcrops in about nine Scottish localities. Prior to the 1970s, *Caloplaca luteoalba* was a common lichen on parkland and wayside elms in its former stronghold of southeast England; today it is almost extinct in England, but has about 15 extant localities in eastern Scotland. This is partly due to the higher survival rate of elms, especially in northeast Scotland, but also to the several occurrences of *C. luteoalba* on the damaged trunks of other trees, especially sycamore. Another species with a close association with elms is sap-groove lichen, *Bacidia incompta*, and this often grew alongside *C. luteoalba*. It too has disappeared from most of England, but is still present in southwest England, growing on the wounded trunks or boughs of other trees, especially ash, beech, field maple and sycamore. Apart from one record from Berwickshire on a wounded beech, *B. incompta* is found in Scotland only on wych elm, and there are now only seven known localities.

The lichen assemblages on elm trunks in open habitats are very different to those seen in woodlands. In open habitats (by roads and tracks, in parklands and along field and woodland margins), the trunks are generally well-lit and enriched by dust or animal excreta. These conditions result in colonisation by numerous, often rather colourful lichens, which grow together to form 'Xanthorion' communities. Characteristic species include several with orange- or yellow-coloured thalli or fruiting bodies, for example the leafy *Xanthoria* species, and crustose species of *Caloplaca* and *Candelariella*. Mixed with these may be species with grey crusty thalli, such as *Amandinea punctata*, *Diplotomma alboatrum*, *Lecanora chlarotera* and *Pertusaria albescens*, as well as those with blue-grey or brown-grey leafy thalli with narrow lobes, belonging to the genera *Phaeophyscia*, *Physcia*, *Physconia* and *Hyperphyscia*. There may also be larger-lobed, leafy lichens such as the grey *Parmelia sulcata* or the brown *Melanelixia subaurifera*, and some

Above: Orange-fruited elm-lichen, *Caloplaca luteoalba*. Image: Mike Sutcliffe.

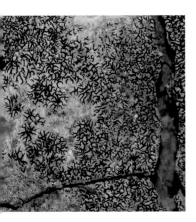

yellow-green shrubby lichens, especially oak moss, *Evernia prunastri*, *Ramalina farinacea* and *R. fastigiata*, but also rarer species such as *Ramalina canariensis*, *R. fraxinea* and *R. lacera*. Where the trunk is leaning, the underside is much drier, and few larger (leafy or shrubby) lichens are found, but this dry habitat is favoured by several species of *Opegrapha*, which have thin, whitish to brownish, crusty thalli and tiny, black script-like or boat-shaped fruiting bodies.

The branches and twigs of elms in open habitats can play host to showy species, such as *Parmelia sulcata*, *Ramalina* and *Xanthoria* species – indeed, such lichens are often more luxuriant on branches than they are on trunks. On the other hand, on twigs and thin branches, one can often find several species better adapted to occurring on smooth bark, such as *Lecanora carpinea*, *L. persimilis* and *Lecidella elaeochroma*, to name just a few, common examples. Less common 'branch specialists' include the leafy lichens *Melanohalea exasperata* and *M. exasperatula*, with brown thalli, and the grey *Parmelina pastillifera*, *Physcia aipolia*, *P. leptalea* and *P. stellaris*.

In the shaded, less nutrient-enriched conditions of woodland, the lichen assemblages on elm trunks look very different. The trees often have a high cover of bryophytes, and the

'moss-free' areas are mainly colonised by rather inconspicuous crustose lichens. In old woodland in high rainfall areas and where the trunks are not in dense shade, there can be a high cover of lichens, especially of those that are able to overgrow bryophytes. These include the large leafy lichens of the genera *Lobaria*, *Nephroma*, *Peltigera*, *Pseudocyphellaria* and *Sticta*, and smaller leafy or scale-like lichens of *Collema*, *Degelia*, *Fuscopannaria*, *Leptogium* and *Parmeliella*. All these are termed 'cyanolichens' as their algal partners are blue-green algae (cyanobacteria), sometimes in addition to a green-algal partner. The blue-green algal partner can fix nitrogen, as well as carbon, from the air, and so these cyanolichens can play an important part in the nitrogen cycle in the woodland ecosystem. Other lichens in such habitats, also often overgrowing bryophytes, include often wide-spreading crustose species such as *Biatora epixanthoides*, *B. sphaeroides* and *Dimerella lutea*. Where bryophytes and larger lichens are not over-dominant, several tiny crustose species characteristic of old-growth woodland can be found, for example *Lecania chlorotiza*, *Piccolia ochrophora*, *Thelopsis rubella*, *Wadeana minuta*, and species in the genera *Agonimia*, *Bacidia*, *Biatoridium*, *Gyalecta*, *Pachyphiale*, *Porina* and *Ramonia*. In drier niches, especially the

Above: *Opegrapha vulgata*, a common 'script lichen'. Image: Mike Sutcliffe.

Below left: Lichen- and moss-covered wych elm on the west coast of Scotland, here with the tree-lungwort, *Lobaria pulmonaria*. Image: RBGE/Brian Coppins.

Below right: *Melanohalea exasperata*, which grows mainly on branches and twigs in open habitats. Image: Mike Sutcliffe.

underside of leaning trunks, *Opegrapha* species may be dominant, and in low rainfall areas several 'pin-head' lichens may occur, especially in bark crevices. These lichens have crustose thalli and tiny stalked fruiting bodies, and include such species as *Chaenotheca hispidula*, *C. trichialis* and the rarer *C. brachypoda*, *C. chlorella* and *C. laevigata*. The 'pin-heads' *Sclerophora pallida* and *S. peronella* occupy old sap runs on wounded trunks.

In the wet and warm (hyperoceanic) conditions of the Western Highlands and Islands, the 'Celtic Rainforest zone', many of the species more characteristic of woodlands can occur in more open habitats, and this area is the stronghold for many of these species in Europe, and in some cases the world.

The table lists 37 lichens that occur on elm in Scotland and are included in the Red Data list for the UK. Under the auspices of the UK Biodiversity Action Plan, several of these species have been provided with action plans and have been the subjects of detailed investigations. A few have also been given special legal protection by being listed on Schedule 8 (and subsequent reviews) of the Wildlife and Countryside Act 1981.

Elm trees provide a home not only for the 37 priority species listed, but also to

Species	Category	S8	o	w
Anaptychia ciliaris	VU		o	
Bacidia circumspecta	VU			w
Bacidia incompta	VU		o	w
Bacidia subincompta	VU			w
Bacidia vermifera	EN			w
Biatoridium delitescens	VU			w
Biatoridium monasteriensis	EN			w
Caloplaca flavorubescens	EN		o	
Caloplaca luteoalba	VU	S8	o	
Chaenotheca chlorella	NT			w
Chaenotheca gracilenta	EN			w
Chaenotheca laevigata	EN			w
Collema fasciculare	NT			w
*Collema fragrans**	EN		o	
Collema nigrescens	NT		o	w
Collema occultatum	NT		o	
Fuscopannaria ignobilis	VU	S8	o	w
Fuscopannaria sampaiana	NT		o	w
Gomphillus calycioides	NT			w
Gyalecta flotowii	NT		o	w
Gyalecta ulmi	EN	S8		w
Heterodermia obscurata	NT			w
Lecanora horiza	NT		o	
Leptogium brebissonii	NT			w
Leptogium cochleatum	VU			w
Leptogium hibernicum	NT			w
Leptogium saturninum	VU		o	w
Pachyphiale fagicola	NT			w
Parmeliella testacea	NT			w
Porina rosei	NT			w
Pyrenula hibernica	VU	S8		w
Ramonia chrysophaea	NT			w
Ramonia dictyospora	NT			w
Sclerophora pallida	VU		o	w
Sclerophora peronella	NT		o	w
Wadeana dendrographa	NT		o	
Wadeana minuta	NT			w

Red Data Book categories:

EN = Endangered
VU = Vulnerable
NT = Near Threatened
S8 = species listed on Schedule 8 (and subsequent reviews) of the Wildlife and Countryside Act 1981
o = in open habitats
w = in woodlands
* = apparently extinct in Scotland

Above: *Caloplaca flavorubescens*, a lichen favouring the trunks of ancient trees, especially of ash and elm in open habitats. Image: Andy Acton.

Left: *Dimerella lutea*, a lichen of humid woodlands, whose distribution extends into the tropics. Image: Mike Sutcliffe.

Right: *Pannaria conoplea*, an attractive species associated with the milder climate of western oceanic woodlands. Image: Sandy Coppins.

Below: *Collema fasciculare*, a cushion-forming 'jelly lichen'. Image: RBGE/Brian Coppins.

many species that, although too common in Scotland to be given a UK Red List status, are of conservation concern in a European or global context. In many old woodland sites, the number of lichens found on elm is usually less than for most other large broadleaved trees. However, this shortfall is often made up for by elm being the only host tree for some 'specials', which require the basic bark qualities provided. The loss of large elms in much of our landscape has meant that several lichens have suffered a severe decline, at least regionally.

This has already been referred to in the cases of *Bacidia incompta* and *Caloplaca luteoalba*, but to these can be added the priority lichens eagle's claws, *Anaptychia ciliaris*, *Bacidia circumspecta*, *Chaenotheca chlorella*, *Collema occultatum*, pale crater lichen, *Gyalecta flotowii*, *Lecanora horiza*, *Pachyphiale fagicola* and *Ramonia dictyospora*. The list does not end there, and the populations of several other species will have suffered a significant regional decline, though not yet to a 'threatened' level in the UK as a whole; examples include *Acrocordia gemmata*, *Agonimia allobata*, *Bacidia rubella*, *Caloplaca ulcerosa*, *Pleurosticta acetabulum*, *Ramalina canariensis* and *Rinodina griseosoralifera*. The threat to some of these lichens is lessened where the habitat is well provided by other tree species that can offer similar conditions, especially our native ash, the introduced Norway maple and the much maligned sycamore.

If you want to get to know more about lichens, a good starting point is the website of The British Lichen Society, where you will find out not only what the Society has to offer, and how you can help, but also links to other sites providing introductory information and illustrations of lichens.

Velvet shank, *Flammulina velutipes*, often occurs in clusters during the winter months. It is commonly found mid-way up a tree. Image: RBGE/Max Coleman.

Death, Decay and New Life

Fungi of Elm

By Roy Watling

Death, Decay and New Life

Fungi of Elm

By Roy Watling

Above: Southern wrinkled peach, *Rhodotus palmatus*, is most prominent on mature dying stag-headed elms or fallen trunks on the soil surface, where it grows in tight clusters. Image: RBGE archive.

Sadly it was with the demise of the wych elm through the ravages of Dutch elm disease that the fungi associated with this tree were brought to the attention of mycologists more than ever before. It was on the remains of elms killed by the disease that a group of less common wood-rotting fungi appeared. One elm fungus, however, had been familiar to mycologists for a long time as it had become a record breaker. A corky, irregularly hoof-shaped fruiting body of *Rigidoporus ulmarius* in the grounds of the former Imperial Mycological Institute at Kew in 1998 measured 171 × 150 × 60 cm with a circumference of 4.9 m. It had an estimated weight of 316 kg, with a 0.1 m increase in circumference over a three-year period. *Rigidoporus* is formed at the base of the tree and has pores beneath the undulating upper surface of the fruiting body. The genus is rather more widespread in the tropics, and *R. ulmarius* is the sole British representative. It may grow on other host trees in other parts of Europe, and is only occasionally found in Scotland.

The most spectacular of the clutch of fungi associated with dying elms is the southern wrinkled peach, *Rhodotus palmatus*, a small shell-pink, shell-shaped, wood-rotting mushroom, which produces droplets on the cap and stem when actively growing. It and the much larger white and hairy capped silky rosegill, *Volvariella bombycina*, are characteristic of elms. The latter mushroom is rare in Scotland and usually grows from wounds. It is related to the padi-straw mushroom, *Volvariella volvacea*, which many people consume in oriental meals. In Kintyre the poplar fieldcap, *Agrocybe cylindracea*, occurs, although not on elm; it is in the south of England that the fungus is more common and although generally on poplar there it also occurs on elms. It is edible and one of the few mushrooms semi-cultivated by the Romans and Moghuls. It is still grown in the traditional way in the Mediterranean and is known as *popilino* there. Another rare and southern mushroom is the elm leech, *Hypsizygus ulmarius*, an oyster mushroom characterised by the development of a distinct mushroom shape topping a stem rather than a shelf or bracket. It and the related, if not identical, *H. tessulatus* occur on large, dead, standing or fallen elms in parkland, along roads, in hedgerows, etc., and is known as far north in the British Isles as the Borders of Scotland.

The common oyster mushroom, *Pleurotus ostreatus*, also occurs on several species of elm and commonly fruits late in the season, but

more specific to elms is the closely related branching oyster, *P. cornucopiae*. The oyster mushroom often accompanies the velvet shank, *Flammulina velutipes*, with its sticky, rubbery, orange cap and dark brown, or even black, velvety stem joined at the base to form clusters. It can often be found in the depth of winter even with snow or hard frost coating the cap. In cultivation it is grown in darkness when it loses all traces of colour and is sold as *enoki*. There are several other common, clustered mushrooms on elm; these include

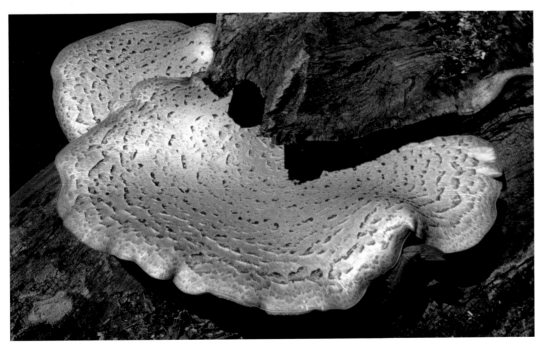

Above: Branching oyster, *Pleurotus cornucopiae*, has ill-formed elongate stems ridged with extensions of the gills and overall cream or buff coloration. It can form large groups of several fruiting bodies joined to a common base. Image: RBGE archive.

Left: Dryad's saddle, *Polyporus squamosus*, is found growing from wounds near the ground and high up in the canopy. Image: RBGE archive.

several inky caps, including the fairy inkcap, *Coprinellus disseminatus*, and *Hypholoma fasciculare*, a mushroom with a purple-brown spore-deposit and sulphur-yellow cap and stem. Both occur on the stumps, chips and debris left after the felling of diseased elms and were especially common at the height of the tragedy. The last is called sulphur tuft, the common name referring to the overall colour, whilst the epithet *fasciculare* refers to its clustered nature. All these species can be found on many other hosts.

Often roadside elms and those in gardens and hedgerows display in the early summer the fruiting bodies of dryad's saddle, *Polyporus squamosus*, especially those trees which have suffered storm or wind damage. Two species of the artist's fungus, *Ganoderma*, occur on elm, especially individual specimen trees in isolation; *G. applanatum* is the rather more widespread on elm in Scotland with *G. australe*, although occurring on this host, more frequent on other trees such as beech. In gardens members of the honey fungus group are widespread and may fruit around the base of a tree under stressed conditions leading to its death.

Above: Brittle cinder, *Ustulina deusta*, is a widespread root rot fungus which forms greyish olive fruiting bodies on the bases of the trunks of trees and blackens with age. Image: RBGE archive.

Armillaria bulbosa is the commonest, although *A. mellea* has been recorded in the books. Careful reassessment is required as to the true identity of some of the marauding *Armillaria* records. Perhaps the true honey fungus on elm is more common in the south of the British Isles than in Scotland.

The roots of elms are universally associated with microscopic fungi, which form what is termed arbuscular endomycorrhiza. Elms are deprived of the colourful, large fruiting bodies found in ectomycorrhizal relationships seen in beeches, birches and oaks. Sadly, therefore, there are no characteristic brittlegills, milkcaps, boletes and the like found with elms. However, elms occur in rather special habitats in nature and these communities do have characteristic fungi. Therefore the specialist host is not the tree but rather the habitat in which it grows. In such plant communities dying elms often show tiers of a whitish bracket fungus usually covered in algae and moss; this is the poplar bracket, *Oxyporus populinus*, which occurs on several species of shade tree, especially poplar and sycamore. As in many areas, depauperate elms in these damp communities are covered over their basal areas by a grey skin with a white or even rose-tinged margin, which gradually takes on an olive cast, and finally darkens to become a black crust. This is brittle cinder, *Ustulina deusta*, now placed in the genus *Kretzschmaria*. Another fungus, the silverleaf fungus, *Chondrostereum purpureum*, which is the scourge of fruit orchards where it causes a decline in fruit trees, also occurs on elms, especially cut ends of trunks. In orchards its presence is indicated by the metallic appearance of the leaves but on elm timber it forms lavender or lilac-purple fruiting bodies. Although often purely acting as a rot fungus it can also cause disease. Two other similarly structured fungi placed in *Stereum*, where *C. purpureum* was once classified, are widespread on elm branches and fallen trunks. These are hairy curtain crust, *Stereum hirsutum*, and bleeding broadleaf crust, *S. rugosum*. The latter, as its common name implies, oozes a red juice when damaged, but don't be misled as the fungus must be actively growing and will not co-operate and 'bleed' if dry. There are no specific crust-fungi on elm; *Athelopsis lembospora*, *Megalocystidium luridum*, *Phanerochaete sordida*, *Radulomyces confluens*, the widespread *Cylindrobasidium evolvens*, elder whitewash, *Lyomyces sambuci*, and split pore-crust, *Schizopora paradoxa*, can all be found on fallen branches of various diameters. *Hyphodontia pruni* appears to prefer decayed bark-free elm in northern Europe and should be looked for in Britain. Three species of *Peniophora*, *P. cinerea* and *P. lycii*, both with purple-grey fruiting bodies, and the rosy crust, *P. incarnata*, all occur on elms but they are even more common on other woody hosts. Amongst the polypores other than those mentioned earlier, those found on elms are widespread on other woody hosts, for example bay polypore, *Polyporus durus*, and blackfoot polypore, *P. leptocephalus*, and various turkeytails, *Trametes* species. Other bracket fungi infrequently seen on elm are more typical of other trees: for example, on oak – mazegill, *Daedalea quercina*, especially in western and northeast Scotland; on goat willow and rowan – cinnamon bracket, *Hapalopilus nidulans*; on goat willow and hazel – hazel bracket, *Skeletocutis nivea*, on the west coast of Scotland especially where the soils are relatively base-rich and wet; and on beech – common mazegill,

Datronia mollis, and smoky bracket, *Bjerkandera adusta*. Except for beech many of these hosts are associated with plant communities which contain wych elm. Although ash is an integral component of some elm communities, only the ubiquitous wood-rotting species *Ceriporia reticulata* appears to transfer between these hosts. *Ceriporia reticulata* possesses shallow pores forming a network which darkens when handled and is found on many deciduous hosts in addition to elm; it even grows on other fungi.

Apart from the last example, which prefers growing on rather old, decaying, wet branches, the crust-fungi and brackets are often more

Above: Turkeytail, *Trametes versicolor*, is recognised by the contrast between the cream-coloured pores beneath and the zoned cap in buffs, browns and blackish or greenish tones edged with white. In South-East Asia it has been used extensively as a medicinal fungus. Image: RBGE archive.

Left: Ear fungus, *Hirneola auricula*, is one of the commonest and most conspicuous jelly fungi in Britain. It probably has a more Atlantic distribution than many other fungi. It is commonest on elder and is edible, and if dry can be easily re-constituted by placing in water. Image: RBGE archive.

conspicuous when on hedgerow plants or those at field margins. They are probably able to grow in such sites because they can withstand the drying conditions which might occur in such habitats, unlike the damp stream-sides and gullies frequented by wych elm under more natural conditions. Jelly fungi are more frequently observed under these humid conditions – examples include small stagshorn, *Calocera cornea*, generally on fallen, horizontal, bark-free trunks; white brain, *Exidia thuretiana*, usually on small diameter branches; and *Exidiopsis calcea*. *Tremella indecorata* recorded on elm branches is in fact growing on another (pyrenomycetous) fungus which may itself be dependent on elm. Where elder grows near to elms the ear fungus, *Hirneola auricula*, has been found fruiting on fallen elm branches, although this is not considered a favoured host.

Wych elms in their natural haunts as indicated grow with other trees to form a fairly closed but low canopy. This supports a humid microclimate and is conducive to the growth

of micro-fungi and those associated with moss-covered limbs, boles and trunks. The latter group includes the minute oysterlings in the genus *Resupinatus*, the toxic *Galerina unicolor* and at least two species of shield fungi, *Pluteus*, especially the willow shield, *P. salicinus*, which occurs on hosts other than elm and the willow suggested by the name. Even less conspicuous may be clusters of bonnet fungi, *Mycena* species, all little bigger than a match head: frost bonnet, *M. adscendens*, *M. meliigena* and *M. pseudocorticola*. On woody trash from elm accumulated on the damp soil beneath the trees the pink-spored *Clitopilus hobsonii* and brown-spored *Crepidotus cesatii* and peeling oysterling, *Crepidotus mollis*, have all been recorded. The much overlooked *Flagelloscypha citrispora* and *Henningsomyces candidus*, both resembling small cup-fungi (discomycetes) more than relatives of the mushrooms, should be looked out for. All of these fungi can be found on a whole range of woody hosts under similar ecological conditions, with *C. mollis* in fact usually found on ash within the elm community, or old specimen trees. On the ground on the strongly organic soils developed along stream-sides in woodlands, especially alluvial plains, the common morel, *Morchella esculenta*, and fluted bird's nest, *Cyathus striatus*, occur. Their cryptic colours make them difficult to find; the morel is a spring fungus.

The woody debris of elm in such sites is best suited for the growth of micro-fungi of which many of the ubiquitous flask- and cup-fungi known as ascomycetous fungi occur on wych elm. These include candle snuff fungus, *Xylaria hypoxylon*, and coral spot, *Tubercularia vulgaris*, the asexual stage of *Nectria cinnabarina*; the last species may even act as a weak parasite. However, four flask-fungi (or pyrenomycetes) can be frequently found each with its own ecological niche. Thus *Anthostoma melanotes*, with large, brown ascospores, grows on bark-less branches; *Cryptosporella hypodermia*, with hyaline, pointed spores, grows in clusters beneath the bark of branches and twigs; and *Lopadostoma gastrinum*, with similar spores to *Anthostoma*, forms black cushions on branches which have fallen and accumulated on wet ground. The distribution and host specificity of the last has been the subject of a study by the author which demonstrates how little we know of the fungi which are associated with a particular elm species. *Quaternaria dissepta*, with

pale brown, sausage-shaped spores, grows on the outer layers of fallen twigs and branches and similar to *Cryptosporella* possesses an asexual stage which often forms before the sexual state develops. *Cryptosporella* is often hidden from view under the bark for all but the late stages of its life cycle when it bursts through in a series of minute, dark caverns holding the sexual stage (perithecia). Similarly, various *Eutypella* species, including the widespread *E. stellulata*, which perhaps specifically grows on the English elm and not the wych elm, grow on dead fallen branches and twigs in a parallel way to *Splanchnonema foedans*, with its large, four-celled, brown spores.

On fallen leaves *Platychora ulmi* is common and is usually preceded by an asexual stage, which has large, four-celled, hyaline conidia. Some discomycetes appear to be confined to fallen, dead elm leaves. Growing on and under bark *Orbilia comma* is often accompanied by *Lachnum deflexum* (formerly *Dasyscyphus*) and the mould *Seiridium intermedium*. Both of the former have only comparatively recently been described as new to science by the diligent collecting and observations of an amateur mycologist, W. D. Graddon. This admirably demonstrates that even today we are a long way from knowing the fungi associated with members of our native flora and there is a lot more work to

Below left: Coral spot, *Nectria cinnabarina*, is also known as the pea stick fungus because it is commonly found on the sticks up which peas and beans are grown. It is a fungus with two very prominent stages, a sexual stage which is dark red and a bright pink asexual stage. Image: RBGE archive.

Below right: Candle snuff fungus, *Xylaria hypoxylon*, gets its name from clouds of spores which are easily dislodged to form a wisp of smoke. Image: RBGE archive.

be undertaken. *Orbilia* and *L. deflexum* were originally found in the Midlands of the UK. There are other fungi occurring on elm leaves but these are active parasites.

Two cup-fungi which appear to be confined to elm branches are the decidedly infrequent, brown, scurfy, cup-shaped *Encoelia siparia* and *Habrostictis rubra*; the latter is also found on dead branches of gorse. It can be found in both spring and autumn but the cup-shaped fruiting bodies (apothecia) are difficult to see under dry conditions and therefore are easily overlooked. Once wet, however, the pink to orange cups are exposed breaking through the bark. The distantly related, spectacular *Sphaerostilbe aurantiaca* (formerly *Nectria*) grows on bark of elm, producing a club-shaped head of asexual spores (conidia) around which the red sexual stage (perithecia) is clustered. It is rare in Britain.

As the ice retreated after the last Ice Age all these fungi, including the ubiquitous species, and both the decomposers and parasites, probably accompanied the elms, which along with other deciduous trees colonised the British Isles to form the wildwood. Some of the fungi would have extended their distribution and travelled northwards to what has been called the Limus Norlandicus, the northern-most migration of oak. However, since Neolithic times in Britain when the elm was preferentially selected for fodder and often

made into hedges, other fungi probably have taken up an association.

Many of the micro-fungi found on wych elm have not been sought for in Scotland with any dedication. For example, *Diplodia melaena*, whose sexual state is the unusual *Cucurbitaria naucosa*, has dark brown, two-celled asexual spores and should be looked for on fallen branches. Lists of 18 different dark-spored moulds which might be recorded with diligent collecting are given in a book by Martin Ellis on dematiaceous hyphomycetes, and 27 coelomycetes (stem and leaf fungi) in two volumes of a now rather dated but nevertheless useful work by Grove. (There is a more modern but not as wide-reaching treatment by Sutton, which must be cross-referenced with Grove.) These books only give an idea of what might occur and probably will ultimately be found not to be exhaustive as many species in all groups are found on elms on the Continent which are not recorded from the British Isles. *Microfungi on Land Plants* by Martin and Pamela Ellis offers a summary of the important micro-forms on elms; included are those species which may be found only in the south of the British Isles. Of the microscopic fungi the scarlet elf cap, *Sarcoscypha austriaca*, growing on mossy logs, is the most spectacular and is the first to greet the New Year.

Above: Silky rosegill, *Volvariella bombycina*, is one of our rarest padi-straw fungi and is found growing out of the softened wood associated with elm wounds. This fungus is so rare it is not known whether it is edible. Image: RBGE archive.

Right: Common oyster mushroom, *Pleurotus ostreatus*, is the oyster mushroom of commerce and is sold widely in supermarkets and served in restaurants labelled 'wild mushroom' although the fungus is actually grown on processed wood debris. Image: RBGE archive.

An elm condemned. Elms in Edinburgh showing symptoms of Dutch elm disease are marked and ring-barked before being felled, to stop the spread of the disease. Image: RBGE/Max Coleman.

Grim Reaper

Elm Disease

By Stephan Helfer

Grim Reaper

Elm Disease

By Stephan Helfer

Below: An elm skeleton in the Scottish Borders stands as a reminder of Dutch elm disease. Image: RBGE/Max Coleman.

The elm has become associated in literature with death and malignancy (see Chapter 3). The earliest link between elm and death appears in Homer's *Iliad*. Homer describes the grave of Eetion being planted with elms. In more recent times the impacts of disease on elms have served to further strengthen the association with death.

Elms, like all trees, play host to a variety of disease-causing organisms. These include fungi, fungus-like organisms, bacteria and viruses. Elms have gained some notoriety for one disease in particular – Dutch elm disease – and inevitably this chapter focuses on the fungal pathogen responsible. Some other common diseases of elms are also dealt with and mention is made of important stress factors that can predispose trees to disease.

Disorders caused by unfavourable environmental conditions can make a tree more vulnerable to disease. In some cases it is difficult to tell what problem came first, an environmental stress or a pathogen, and in many cases each appears to enhance or modify the effect of the other.

Wych elm is well adapted to the British lowland climate. It prefers the northwestern parts of the British Isles and is the only native elm in Ireland. However, there are some climatic extremes that it cannot tolerate. In particular excess water may starve the tree roots of oxygen and predispose plants to attack by disease. Conversely, drought can lead to leaf loss and reduced terminal growth. Drought-stressed elms are also more prone to invasion by elm bark beetles with its accompanied risk of Dutch elm disease. Both high and low temperatures are more harmful when unseasonal than in their own right, and elms particularly suffer from late frosts.

In addition to the above natural stresses, humans provide further sources of stress in the form of chemicals, such as de-icing salt, and poisons, such as herbicides or leaking gas pipes, as well as pollution in many different guises.

Climate and environmental stresses, pests and living pathogens do not occur in isolation and often act in concert or in sequence, leading to disease complexes and epidemic synergies, where no one original problem cause can be identified. Furthermore, even pathogens themselves are prone to infection by diseases through hyper parasites and viruses and this can moderate disease outcomes.

European elms are host to more than 250 species of parasitic fungi. This includes some fleshy fungi, such as honey fungus, as well as many microscopic fungi, for example powdery mildew, leaf spot fungi and Dutch elm disease. The majority of elm diseases are caused by true fungi (Mycota), but some ailments are caused by downy mildew related organisms (Oomycota such as *Phytophthora* or *Pythium*).

Root diseases of elms in Europe are restricted to those caused by *Armillaria* species, *Rhizoctonia solani*, *Phytophthora cambivora* and *Pythium intermedium*. Only *Armillaria* is a serious pathogen of mature trees, the others being mainly seedling root problems or weakness pathogens. Currently elms are not known to

be host to the dreaded *Phytophthora ramorum* or *P. kernoviae* pathogens that cause the disease known as sudden oak death and are root pathogens in many other hosts under natural conditions. However, experimental results using detached leaves in the laboratory showed susceptibility of English elm to the latter pathogen. Given the huge host range of the pathogens in question, it would not be surprising if all elms, including wych elm, were to be seriously affected by them in the future, under fitting environmental conditions.

Both root and wilt diseases are particularly damaging for trees, as they affect the survival of long-lasting structures (stems, branches and roots). Wilt diseases cause wilting and death of foliage through interruption of the flow of water through the vascular system of the plant. Among the wilt diseases, which include Dutch elm disease, are at least two general wilt diseases, affecting many different host plants. The fungal pathogens *Phaeostalagmus tenuissimus* (formerly known as *Verticillium tenuissimum*) and *Dothiorella sarmentorum* have been isolated from elms affected by wilt. Both fungi appear to be of minor importance in Europe. Other species of *Verticillium* are known to cause vascular wilts in elms in the USA, notably the blue stain

Far left: Elm in Inverleith Park, Edinburgh in May 2005. Image: RBGE/Max Coleman.

Left: The same tree all but killed by Dutch elm disease in July 2005. Image: RBGE/Max Coleman.

fungus *V. albo-atrum* which also is well known for soil-borne vascular wilt diseases of many woody plants in Britain and Europe. Compared with Dutch elm disease, these diseases are of relatively low importance.

Another kind of disease is the formation of cankers. These are localised areas of dead wood or bark and underlying layers caused by the presence of a pathogen, and should not be confused with burr-wood, where no pathogen is required. They develop from an initial infection (normally through a wound) and can reach considerable size, weakening any limbs they grow on. Large cankers can lead to branch or stem failure through mechanically disrupting healthy wood. Moreover, cankers can kill the cells responsible for nutrient flow (phloem), girdle limbs and cause starvation of parts of the affected tree. In Europe cankers on elm are most frequently caused by fungi of the genus *Nectria*, including *N. cinnabarina*, the common coral spot fungus.

On top of the more serious structural pathogens affecting the wood tissues, elms are also hosts of many foliar pathogens. While they cause damage and loss of photosynthesis, these pathogens tend to be less important since the

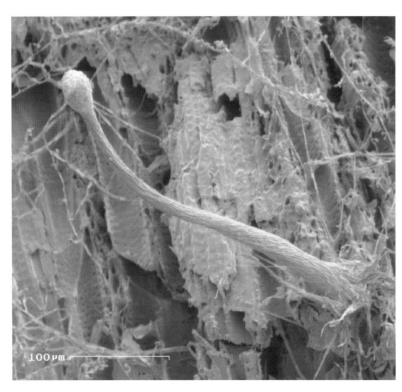

100 µm

leaves are lost in the autumn in any case. There are at least 50 species of fungi known to affect the leaves of elms in Europe, North America and Asia. Many of these are more general foliar pathogens of trees but some are specific to elm. An example is the powdery mildew *Erysiphe clandestina*, which is restricted to living elm leaves and has recently been rediscovered in central Europe. Even though most foliar pathogens only cause mild symptoms, this can be enough to exacerbate other stresses and render the trees vulnerable to more serious pests and diseases.

The vascular wilt disease of elms caused by *Ophiostoma ulmi*, commonly known as Dutch elm disease, was first discovered in north-central Europe around 1910. Between 1919 and 1934 its cause was researched by Dutch scientists and this is where the name originates. From the late 1920s on Dr Tom Peace began monitoring its rapid spread through Britain, where it had been accidentally introduced around 1927. In 1930 it was introduced to North America, carried in elm logs that were destined for the production of veneer. As North American elms were highly susceptible to the disease, and elm bark beetles that could spread the disease were naturally present, the fungus spread steadily into all areas where elms grew naturally or had been planted. This epidemic is still ongoing and has seen little if any decline since the first arrival of the pathogen.

After killing an estimated 10-40% of elm trees in several European countries the first epidemic died down, and in 1960 Peace concluded that "unless it completely changes its present trend of behaviour, it will never bring about the disaster once considered imminent". However, such a change of behaviour was exactly what was going to happen in the following year. An aggressive strain of the disease, later to be identified as a new species, *Ophiostoma novo-ulmi*, appeared on the scene. Two subspecies were recognised: one was centred in the region of Moldova in Romania (the European subspecies), whilst the other simultaneously appeared in the southern Great Lakes region of North America, and was named subspecies *americana*. This species was far more aggressive on both European

Dutch Elm Disease in Edinburgh

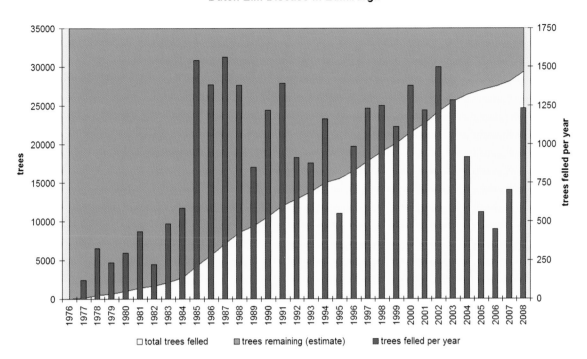

and American elms. During the 1960s it was spread throughout the elm populations of Europe, mainly on infected timber, and since then has been responsible for the death of over 25 million mature elms in the UK alone. In affected areas the elm population has been reduced to a mixture of seedlings and suckers that are knocked back by the disease on a cycle of 10 to 15 years. Rare survivors of the disease do exist in most areas and some populations of wych elm in the north and west of Scotland remain unaffected by the disease.

Although some efforts at stemming the progress of the first epidemic were made in North America, especially in New York City, most control measures were given up with the upheavals of the Second World War. In Britain there was an attempt to stop the progress of the second epidemic under the Plant Health Act 1967, and through specific legislation in the form of the Dutch Elm Disease (Local Authorities) Order 1984. This gave local authorities powers of inspection and notification for sanitation felling of affected trees and to enforce restrictions of movement of infected timber (bark). Since 1988 only a defined number of local authorities have

retained powers under this act. Both Edinburgh and Brighton still use the powers to protect their remaining elm populations which are of considerable landscape value. Nevertheless, Edinburgh has suffered great losses in its elm population. Many of the lost elms have been replaced by limes, sycamore and smaller trees such as rowan or bird cherry that lack the stature or specimen tree appeal of elms.

Despite being situated near the City Council's lumber-yard where elm logs are everyday occurrences, and also being near several foci of infection, the Royal Botanic Garden Edinburgh has managed to keep a number of the elms in its collection. Even so,

Above: Graph showing the impact of Dutch elm disease in Edinburgh despite disease management being conducted. In other affected areas of the UK, almost all trees died within the first decade of the epidemic. Image: RBGE/Stephan Helfer.

Left: Diseased elms become breeding sites for elm bark beetles. Image: Forestry Commission Picture Library.

almost half (22 of 46) of the original trees at the Edinburgh Garden have gone today. Of those remaining 14 are considered susceptible to Dutch elm disease and ten resistant. The wych elm that gave rise to the Wych Elm Project was one of the casualties. The tree had been carefully monitored over many years and subject to fungicide injections to try to prevent the disease taking hold. Similarly, of the 24 accessions originally planted at Benmore Botanic Garden in Argyll, 13 are still alive.

Parts of the Scottish Highlands, Argyll and Bute and the Islands are still largely free of disease, and Inverness still maintains a control strategy at the crossroads in relation to the wych elm populations in the north and west of Scotland.

Dutch elm disease is dependent on bark beetle vectors for infection of healthy trees in new neighbourhoods. Locally the disease can also spread through root grafts, a common phenomenon in field elms in hedgerows, but not so common in wych elm. Whereas there are around 11 bark beetle species potentially spreading Dutch elm disease worldwide, in Britain only two species are implicated as disease vectors: *Scolytus scolytus* and *S. multistriatus*. These beetles feed on

elms and bore into the bark of mature elms to lay their eggs in characteristic brood galleries. For the disease to be carried from a diseased elm to a healthy tree there must be a connection between breeding beetles and the production of spores by the fungus. Fungal colonies tend to produce asexual and sexual spores in cavities in and under the bark. The brood galleries of the beetles are ideal cavities for spore production. As mature beetles emerge from the breeding area, they may carry fungal spores on their bodies, which they then may take to new trees on which they feed.

Investigations have shown that not all beetles emerging from infected elms carry spores, and some only very few. However, this is little comfort, as only a few spores are necessary to infect a healthy tree. Once successful infection has occurred, the fungus spreads through the water-conducting vessels of the tree. Small, white, oval spores are formed in clusters on short strands of fungal cells. These spores are carried passively in the vessels, occasionally reproducing by budding, settling on the vessel walls and producing a fungal web. During this phase the fungus produces enzymes and toxins which damage the vessel wall cells and lead to the production of

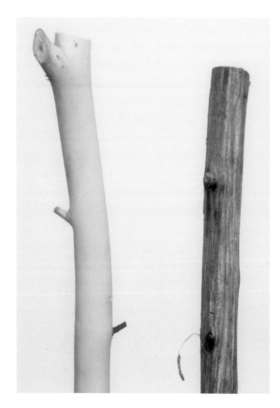

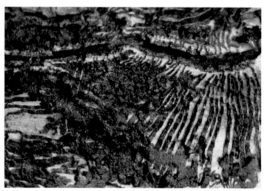

Right: Brown staining of a diseased elm twig (right) compared to a healthy twig (left) after removing the bark. Image: Forestry Commission Picture Library/Thelma Evans.

Far right top: Characteristic breeding galleries of elm bark beetles. Image: RBGE archive.

Far right bottom: Stem cross-section showing discoloration of the water-conducting cells due to fungal toxins. Image: Forestry Commission Picture Library/Thelma Evans.

overgrown lining tissue cells, so-called tyloses, as well as gum from decaying cells, which will in due course block up the water-conducting vessels. The blockage leads to the characteristic wilt symptom and the whole tree may die in a matter of weeks. The death of water-conducting vessels leads to an additional symptom: dark streaking immediately under the bark.

The fungus then proceeds to produce a second generation of asexual spores. In dying or recently dead trees the fungal threads invade and colonise the bark cells and form 1 - 2 mm long, hair-like fruiting structures with thousands of sticky spores exuded from the end. These and sexual reproductive flask-shaped structures (perithecia), which also exude spores, grow inside hollow spaces in the bark, the beetle breeding galleries being ideal in position and size. Beetle vectors pick up spores from within the bark and the infection cycle is complete.

As with many other plant diseases, by far the most important vector for long-distance disease spread is man. Infected elm wood imported from North America was the means by which the highly aggressive strain reached Europe. Endless undocumented shipping of wood across and between continents is likely the cause for many new outbreaks in up-to-then disease-free areas.

One of the main aims of successful control of Dutch elm disease must be the management of its vectors. Quarantine measures, timely removal of infected trees and restrictions on the movement of untreated timber are some of the most promising control strategies where this is possible. It has been shown that the prompt removal of infected trees is in fact less expensive than delaying removal until the disease has had a chance to spread. These control and management strategies require careful tree monitoring by experienced arboriculturists. Many local authorities employ tree specialists with the particular task of monitoring Dutch elm disease. An outbreak in New Zealand in 1989 was eradicated successfully by 1999. After the initial infection was detected, all elms in the vicinity were monitored and diseased trees removed speedily. The fungus probably had entered through beetles in infected packaging material from Europe.

Many trees were injected with fungicide to prevent establishment of the fungus; however, this control has proved impractical in most situations. Image: Forestry Commission Picture Library/Thelma Evans.

Above: Yellow foliage is an indicator of the initial stages of Dutch elm disease infection high in the canopy.
Image: RBGE/Max Coleman.

The removal of infected trees can be combined with targeted cultural strategies involving mixed planting and the avoidance of root graft formation by either disrupting existing grafts or planting trees at greater distances. In the past insecticides have been used to control the beetle vectors. Being expensive, not particularly effective and endangering other wildlife such as bees and useful insects as well as people, their use is now discontinued. The use of fungicide to protect specimen trees from infection has been practised with mixed results. The elms at the Edinburgh Garden were treated in this manner. Fungicide was applied through small holes drilled into the base of the tree; these were then sealed until further treatment in the following years. This in itself was risky, as other problems could arise (including adverse reaction of the tree to the chemical or effects on mycorrhizal fungi), and as it is both expensive and not completely effective it was not continued here. For some large and valuable specimen trees it is still an option.

Other options for Dutch elm disease control involve biological control measures such as the use of viruses harmful to the fungus, the so-called 'd-factors'. The one challenging aspect is the rapid spread and huge reproductive potential of the fungus. Any successful virus will likely 'breed' its own resistance in the fungus population, as it causes high selective pressure for resistance to itself. Options to genetically manipulate d-factor viruses are being considered but more research is necessary to investigate possible side effects.

The most promising option for future elm generations is the establishment of a diverse population of elms with various resistance characters against the fungus. In the past many urban street tree plantings were of uniform plant material, which brought with it the danger of monocultures as well as the doubtfully desirable effects of uniformity. These monocultures present themselves to a pathogen as one big organism, quickly leading to adaptations in infective potential, and often leading to devastating epidemics. To overcome this danger, diversification is the best policy. There are many groups working on the breeding of elms which have enhanced resistance to Dutch elm disease as well as desirable growth habits, necessary hardiness, frost resistance and other important characteristics.

So, is there a future for elms after Dutch elm disease? Several initiatives in resistant breeding have shown promising results. Cultivars released so far have shown varying degrees of resistance or tolerance (the fungus develops but does not kill the tree) to the pathogen. Some cultivars, like 'Urban', showed initial promise only to be found less wind resistant than necessary for the British climate. However, there are numerous elm clones available for planting, with new ones being bred, and the chances are that replacements will be found. One word of warning, though: should the perfect tree be found and marketed, then it is only a matter of time before it too will succumb to a devastating pest or disease, if it is planted in monoculture over large areas. The extreme vulnerability of English elm results from its genetic uniformity. We need to learn the lesson that disease epidemics teach us: genetic diversity is the key to adaptation and long-term survival.

Phoenix Tree
Recovery from Dutch Elm Disease
By Max Coleman

The dwarf cultivar 'Nana' is relatively safe from Dutch elm disease as elm bark beetles tend to feed at a greater height above ground. Image: RBGE/Max Coleman.

Phoenix Tree
Recovery from Dutch Elm Disease

By Max Coleman

The subtle maroon haze of an elm in full flower was once the backdrop to many a walk in February and March. To see this early herald of spring now requires determination and more than a little local knowledge.

Dutch elm disease was one of the major plant disease epidemics of the 20th century (see Chapter 7). The effect on the British landscape and the national psyche has been profound. At least two organisations, the Conservation Foundation and the Tree Council, came into being in response to the devastating loss of trees and a feeling that something needed to be done.

During the first half of the 20th century there were outbreaks of the disease in Europe and North America. These led to efforts to identify the cause of the disease and the scientific detective work involved merits a book in itself. In 1921 Marie Beatrice Schwarz finally isolated the fungal agent of the disease. She was one of seven Dutch female plant pathologists who carried out early work on the disease, which is why we know it as 'Dutch' elm disease.

The severity of the early outbreaks proved to be minor in comparison to the virulent strain of the disease that arrived in Britain in the late 1960s. During the 1970s Dutch elm disease came dramatically into the public eye as it ravaged the elm population of England. The strain which caused the 1970s outbreak, later identified as a new species (see Chapter 7), has turned out to be both highly contagious and lethal to all of the European elms. Since initial entrance at south coast ports the disease has been travelling north through Britain to areas previously unaffected; detailed monitoring of losses is no longer carried out.

Reviewing developments over the last 40 years it is hard to believe that the prospects for elms are remotely positive. The mood at

Above: Newly sprouted hardwood cuttings. Image: RBGE/Lynsey Wilson.

Right: Despite the careful control measures carried out by the City of Edinburgh Council elms are lost every year. Image: Edinburgh Evening News.

EVENING NEWS   www.edinburghnews.com

Five trees axed a day in city as Dutch Elm Disease takes its toll

Removal forced by spread of deadly fungal condition

■ ANDREW PICKEN
Council Reporter

FIVE of the Capital's trees are being felled every day as council chiefs battle with the ravages of Dutch Elm Disease spreading through the city's woodlands.

Just under 10,000 council-owned trees have been chopped in the last five years, with around half of those being cut because of the fungal disease attacking the city's elm trees.

Council tree surgeons are forced to remove the trees carrying Dutch Elm Disease on safety grounds.

But other reasons for the city's trees being chopped include when they are causing damage to prop-

The 'Achievement Tree' at
Kaimes School takes shape with
the assistance of Tammie Severn,
pupil. Pupils made the tree
with the help of Chris Holmes
and Sharon Kirkby.
Image: RBGE/Amy Copeman.

Celebrating
a Life

Wych Elm Community Projects

By Ian Edwards

Celebrating a Life

Wych Elm Community Projects

By Ian Edwards

Below: Max Coleman helps Kaimes School pupils plant a young wych elm at Chris Holmes' Gogar workshop. Image: Lawrence Tierney.

"This elm is so old it was here, in this spot, before the Botanic Garden. It was here before the City of Edinburgh came this far and there were woods all along the Water of Leith. It may even be descended from the ancient wildwood that once covered most of Scotland... Just think of what scenes have taken place beneath this tree – the fights, the trysts, the games, the stories told and secrets shared."

This was how the Garden's wych elm was introduced to hundreds of schoolchildren from all over Scotland, who took part in the Scottish Trees programme. Admittedly this exaggerated the antiquity of the tree, but there is no reason why its lineage should not go back to the wildwood. And, reassuringly, there is also no reason why it shouldn't extend into the future. There are plenty of young seedlings, offspring of the original tree no doubt, growing within its former shadow. Pupils learnt how to estimate the height of the tree – by looking backwards through their legs until they could just see the top of the tree, then measuring the distance to the trunk. They encircled its giant girth, rubbed its bark, printed its leaves and collected handfuls of its prolific seed to demonstrate wind dispersal.

This well-loved tree was also used as the model for Scotland's largest (albeit temporary) stained-glass window. During the autumn of 1994, artists Mary Walters and Kate Downie took the image of the tree as a template for filling the windows of the Edinburgh City Council office buildings that stood on the corner of the Royal Mile and George IV Bridge. Working from Kate's drawings more than 200 schoolchildren helped to create a mosaic that covered 180 square metres. When the lights were turned on inside the offices the tree appeared, larger than life and in glorious summer green, shining out over the streets of the Old Town. Sadly, little remains of that spectacle now – most of the records are lost and even the building has been demolished and a new one is being constructed on the site. Only a single drawing, by Kate Downie, seems to have survived.

4 seasons.

Wych Elm

the branches fall away from the stem
like water tumbling over rocks
a rough cascade

Much wider Paper. Same Depth
Blue/Grey ceterlem wash.
Acrylic White
Green grey a Parchment White
Acrylic Green Black + Ink
36 x Kodak film. 50 mm lense
Pentel MICRO - Correct

details
leaves
attached + fallen
trunk showers

enclosure
Downie 94

Having stood so long as a prominent landmark of the Edinburgh Garden it was a sad day when the giant was declared as diseased and unsafe. Although there had been several attempts to inject the tree against Dutch elm disease, the infection spread quickly and nothing could be done to save it. The decision was taken to have the timber sawn into boards and to have it transformed into beautiful furniture and other hand-crafted pieces by some of Scotland's top craftsmen and women. In this way the dead tree would be given a new lease of life in the homes of some of its many admirers.

The bark was removed and burnt while the main body of the tree was taken to Lothian Trees and Timber sawmill at Cousland. I think we had all expected this huge tree would have a hollow core but the wood was sound through to the centre. It was also clear as the saw sliced the main trunk into boards that the slow growth of its mature years had created some close-grained timber with very interesting patterning. Once it had been dried in the kiln the boards were displayed in the sawmill. A number of prospective makers and their clients came to view the wood. In this way we hoped that the tree itself would inspire and inform some of the designs.

Meanwhile we began to search for support for the exhibition and film that were to be core elements of the Wych Elm Project. The Scottish Arts Council were interested in the potential the exhibition had for promoting Scottish crafts and encouraging people to consider commissioning original pieces rather than buying mass-produced furniture, and they agreed to be sponsors. Scottish Natural Heritage could appreciate the value in promoting one of Scotland's most important but often forgotten species of native tree. They were also keen on the environmental message about recycling material and responsible use of natural resources. However, they were most enthused by the potential for community involvement in the Wych Elm Project and it was this element that they chose to support.

Initially we had agreed to carry out three community projects as part of the Wych Elm

Above: Kate Downie's original drawing of the Garden's wych elm was used as inspiration for a community art project. Image: RBGE/Lynsey Wilson.

Project but there was so much enthusiasm that we decided to stretch this to four. Two of these were carried out in partnership with Newbattle Abbey College and Forestry Commission Scotland, and took place in Lord Ancrum's Wood near Dalkeith, Midlothian; one project involved building the Wych Elm Yurt and the other was an arts project involving music, poetry and song. The third project was to create an 'Achievement Tree' at Kaimes School in Edinburgh, a collaboration with Chris Holmes and Sharon Kirkby from Gogar Cabinetworks. The final project included storytelling, music and woodwork with Fife woodworker Kenny Grieve and children of Alva Primary School.

Newbattle Abbey College is a residential college with adult students of all ages and from a wide range of backgrounds. Although they arrive with a variety of life skills they are without formal academic training and sometimes lack confidence. The year they spend at Newbattle can be a life-changing experience and many of the graduates go on to university or higher education. Many of the students are not used to sitting inside being lectured to, and ecology lecturer Stephanie Walker likes to make use of the neighbouring Lord Ancrum's Wood for

practical lessons. The woods are managed in partnership with Forestry Commission Scotland, and the Woodland Wardens, Roddy McTavish and Miranda Grant, also took an active part in the community projects run at the College.

In Lord Ancrum's Wood students normally learn species recognition and the uses of the different native trees. However, the yurt project took this a stage further. Under the supervision of Paul Millard of Red Kite Yurts the students gained practical experience of harvesting and working the different timbers (wych elm, ash, maple and oak) that made up the frame of a beautiful 3.5 m diameter Kyrgyzstan-style yurt. Paul was able to involve the students in all stages of the process, from selecting suitable trees in the wood to cutting, shaping and finishing them. He even invited the students to his workshop in Stirlingshire where he set up a steam box so that they could bend the long curved ash and maple poles that make up the roof structure. A further challenge, involving the combined strength of several members of the team, was the creation of the wheel-like centrepiece that is constructed from steam-bent pieces of oak. Over the ten

weeks of the yurt project the participants not only discovered new skills but many also found their confidence and ability to work as part of a team were developed through the experience.

The door of the yurt, made entirely from wood from the Garden's wych elm, was created by Paul in his workshop. His research for this piece took him to Kyrgyzstan, the home of the yurt. Details of the door, including the latch and the horse-head tensioners, are faithful copies of those he saw in the homes of his hosts during his travels. Now complete with cover, groundsheet and the all-important woodstove the yurt has begun its travels around the country as the perfect venue for music and storytelling sessions.

The following year a new group of Newbattle Abbey College students took part in another project, working with Savourna Stevenson, one of Scotland's most influential composers, and the Edinburgh Makar (poet laureate to the city) Valerie Gillies. Although the big old elms at the College have all succumbed to Dutch elm disease, the woodlands still contain many young wych elm trees that have not been infected. These

provided the starting point for a series of workshops to explore the history, folklore and uses of wych elm in Scotland through the media of poetry, music and song. For many of the participants it was the first time they had been given the opportunity to be creative in this way.

The arched interior walls of the 12th-century Abbey's crypt created a suitable 'folk-cellar' atmosphere for the sounds of drum, guitars, harp and voice. Accomplished musicians and

Above: Paul Millard with the Wych Elm Yurt. The door is made from the Garden's wych elm. Image: Michael Brooks.

Left: Detail of lock on the Wych Elm Yurt wooden door. Image: Michael Brooks.

beginners worked with Valerie and Savourna who performed poetry and harp music, shared their research and nurtured the creativity within the group. Two original songs, written in a traditional style, were recorded in the sound recording studios of the Jewel and Esk College. Another output of the project was a collection of six poems on the wych elm theme. This poem by Sandra Swanney was inspired by the wych elm:

Above and right: Community project workshops led by Valerie Gillies and Savourna Stevenson at Newbattle Abbey College. Images: Stephanie Walker.

The Wych Elm and Me

You stand so tall and proud
I come to you for strength and wisdom
Your branches welcome me
Your spirit invites me
You give me hope

So clear that you are holding my hand

I can hear your voice
I can hear it in the wind as you speak
You hold me close
Red heartwood full of joy
You fill my heart

So clear that you are holding my hand

Fed by the sun and rain
Fruit carried on the breeze
Connects all living things
A love that we all long for
You feed my spirits

So clear that you are holding my hand

The Kaimes School 'Achievement Tree' was a unique project that combined the skills of two highly experienced professional cabinet makers with the enthusiasm and energy of the pupils and staff of an Edinburgh special school. The inspiration for the project came from Mary Walters, a teacher at Kaimes, who had been involved in the earlier wych elm project at the Council offices on George IV Bridge. It was Mary who suggested the partnership with leading cabinet maker Chris Holmes, and Chris who enlisted the support of Sharon Kirkby, a colleague from Gogar Cabinetworks. Together they came up with an idea for a tree sculpture on which the children could hang leaves that represented their achievements within the school. An ideal place was found for the tree in the corridor outside the new library. The school's Craft, Design and Technology teacher Lawrence Tierney took a leading role in managing the pupils' involvement.

Outside boards were selected for the form of the tree. These were quite tree-like in appearance to begin with and rather than hide the natural shape of the tree in a piece of refined cabinet making it was decided to retain and enhance as much of the original beauty as possible – in effect to 'build a tree out of the wood'. Initial construction was done at Gogar Cabinet-works and then the pieces were taken to the school where the children were able to sculpt and finish the work. Many of the Kaimes pupils find language and communication challenging and may be marginalised from mainstream events in the wider community. However, they responded enthusiastically to the project and brought the final shape and figure out of the wood.

The Achievement Tree has become an invaluable resource within the school and is used to recognise the pupils' developing confidence and self-esteem. It is a tribute to all involved that the pupils played such a major role in creating the Achievement Tree.

The fourth community project was developed and executed by Fife-based green woodworker Kenny Grieve. Kenny is a familiar figure at wood fairs and other events across the country where he can usually be seen turning on his pole-lathe and spinning a story or two at the same time!

Above: Leaves representing individual pupils' achievements are added to the Achievement Tree at Kaimes School. Image: RBGE/Amy Copeman.

Left: Leaves on the Achievement Tree. Image: RBGE/Amy Copeman.

Far left: Kaimes School artwork. Image: RBGE/Amy Copeman.

For the Wych Elm Project he chose to work with Alva Primary School in Clackmannanshire. The pupils took stories about Scottish trees as a starting point for creating their own tree stories and songs. 'Old Crouvie', a story from the repertoire of Aberdeenshire traveller and master storyteller Stanley Robertson, and 'The Tale of a Stick', an original tale by the pupils themselves, were further developed as performance pieces. Development began with 'mind maps' and the pupils went on to create scripts and costumes. Under Kenny's guidance they even made their own wooden musical instruments, from clap sticks to xylophones, to provide percussion accompaniment. The particular qualities of different woods, including the wych elm, were considered and tested experimentally. Ultimately the two plays were performed in front of the whole school, as part of Alva Primary School's celebration of Earth Day on 22 April 2008.

Although they were each very different, all of the community projects shared a feeling of celebration for one of Scotland's most important, yet often overlooked, native trees. They all involved professional craftspeople or artists working directly with participants and provided hands-on experience for everyone involved. In all cases participants were encouraged and inspired to explore new areas, learn new skills or develop creative ideas. The workshop leaders and professional artists and craftspeople also showed considerable skill at bringing out talent in others and helping boost confidence and self-esteem.

Above: Alva Primary School's celebration of Earth Day included a project to make and play wooden instruments.
Image: Kenny Grieve.

Right: Alva Primary School artwork.
Image: Alva Primary School.

There is no doubt that at the end of these projects all the participants have a much deeper understanding and appreciation of the wych elm tree and the very important part it has played in Scotland's past. They have learned about the threat to elms across the country and have come to appreciate that, at least for the time being, parts of Scotland remain as strongholds of this beautiful and versatile tree. All the participants were touched in some way by the tree and its place in our heritage.

In contrast to the exhibition pieces (see Chapter 10) the community projects were about learning: processes rather than products. However, there were significant outputs from the projects, including the Wych Elm Yurt, Kaimes' Achievement Tree, musical instruments, poems, songs, a CD and an inspiring documentary film. The Royal Botanic Garden Edinburgh is especially grateful to all the workshop leaders, artists, craftspeople and others who contributed their time and energy to the projects and helped make them such a big success, and also to Bonnie Maggio, Julie Forrest and their colleagues at Scottish Natural Heritage for advice and support throughout.

Meet the Makers
The Wych Elm Project Exhibition

By Ian Edwards and Peter Toaig

Ian Grant working wych elm.
Image: RBGE/Amy Copeman.

Meet the Makers

The Wych Elm Project Exhibition

By Ian Edwards and Peter Toaig

Below: Clients and makers viewing the planked wood at Lothian Trees and Timber sawmill. Image: Michael Brooks.

At the time of writing (December 2008) 22 artists were either working on, or had completed, commissions for the Wych Elm Project. Of these, half are furniture makers and the others represent a variety of arts and craft-based activities, from sculpture, jewellery, toymaking, letter-carving and screen-printing to hand-crafted fishing rods. Together they represent a diverse range of Scotland's best designers, artists and craftspeople. The variety of their approaches, styles and influences is immense but the one element they share is an enthusiasm for wych elm and in particular the much-loved and sadly missed wych elm tree which grew at the Royal Botanic Garden Edinburgh until it had to be felled in 2003.

The making of fine furniture from elm is always a challenge, but this particular tree provided more difficulties than most. A woodland tree is constrained by the sunlight available and grows towards this light. The Garden's elm grew in open conditions and formed a broad crown.

The wood contained knots, splits, tears, areas of rot and wildly varying grain – features which were either to be overcome, removed or occasionally exploited by the makers involved. In addition, the timber of elm is highly resilient and likely to blunt tools used in woodworking more quickly than any other native species. The difficulties of working with elm are compensated by the extraordinarily rich colour and texture which are a feature of the finished work.

Changing fashions in the use of timber species have varied with decorative style itself. In the past, wych elm was shunned as a timber for fine furniture not just because it was hard to work, but also because the 'wildness' of the grain was generally perceived as being unsophisticated and crude (see Chapter 4). In the same way that Victorian train passengers passing through the Alps would draw their curtains to avoid the perceived ugliness of the untamed mountains, elm wood did not serve an idealised notion of beauty. Into the 20th century, most interior design styles still were not well suited to the use of elm. Through the sensual forms of Art Nouveau, geometric lines of Art Deco, sleek modernism and lurid use of plastics of the 1960s, elm was never in vogue (being perceived as too rustic). It has arguably been only in the last 25 years that society has entertained a more carefree attitude, and developed a taste for unconformity in its use of decor. Coincidentally, the wave of Dutch elm disease heading north through Britain came to Scotland at this time – just as fashion took this turn towards the organic – and Scotland's furniture makers found an abundance of suitable raw material and a market that had not existed before (see Chapter 4).

Of those artist makers first to recognise this new opportunity, Tim Stead, and the furniture he produced in his workshop in the Scottish Borders, clearly stood out. His name became synonymous with bold, heavy, asymmetric slabs of elm containing as design features the very flaws that had repulsed previous generations – features now to be celebrated. One of Tim's many legacies

is the high esteem in which wych elm is now held among Scotland's woodworkers.

Chris Holmes is another long-established maker who has worked with wych elm for many years. He neatly summarises the difficulties and pleasures of working with this wood:

> It is a tough timber and for ... a cabinet maker who usually works with fine wood, it poses its own challenges. It is a wild timber with a grain pattern that is quite spectacular. On the negative side, it is never a quiet timber – it is tough on machines, and on cutters, and continues to move once the piece has been made.

To minimise this natural obstinacy in the wood, every component part in every piece made for the Wych Elm Project exhibition was carefully selected from the tree, so that the grain complemented its shape and suited its position within the piece. This made it possible for the wildness of the grain to be incorporated into the design to provide not only strength but beauty.

Above: Chris Holmes with pieces of elm from the Kaimes School project. Image: Lawrence Tierney.

Sam grew up in a creative environment –
his parents have a woodcarving and gilding
business – and from an early age Sam was
drawn to the beauty of wood. His family is based
near Langholm in Eskdalemuir, Dumfriesshire,
close to the Samye Ling Tibetan Buddhist
monastery. Sam is a passionate rock climber
and mountaineer, and has led several climbing
expeditions in the Himalaya. Much of his work
appears to be influenced by the gentle, uplifted
curves, geometric shapes and play of light
that are characteristic of traditional Himalayan
architecture. Sam also trained for a period with
the Derbyshire master craftsman Andrew Lawton
before setting up his own workshop and
developing his own distinctive style.

Sam described his piece for the Wych
Elm Project as "the perfect commission".
He was keen to work with wych elm because
of its swirling grain and fantastic colours.
The timber from the Garden's wych elm had the
most decorative grain he had ever encountered,
making it ideal for his vision of a simple piece
where interesting wood could dominate.
The commission – a table – was intended for the
entrance hall of the client's house so Sam wanted
to make the piece as welcoming as possible:
"an abstract figure with outstretched arms was an
image I worked with and drew inspiration from".
His greatest challenge was to preserve the integrity
of a living tree that had been reduced to slabs of
wood; to achieve this he "shaped the boards into
simple forms whilst trying to retain the original
arrangement of the wood in the tree".

Images: RBGE/Amy Copeman.

Caroline Cloughley

Caroline graduated from Edinburgh College of Art in 2004, and since then her distinctive butterfly jewellery has appeared in a number of exhibitions and featured in articles in the fashion pages of newspapers and magazines.

Drawing from her own lepidopterophobia, a deep-rooted fear of the seemingly harmless butterfly, her work juxtaposes its overtly feminine motif with dramatic horror film stills, reflecting both her personal terror and the popular love of its exquisite form. Caroline uses carefully selected, apposing materials, such as precious metals with laminated paper or freshwater pearls with acetate, to illustrate this dichotomy.

In her Wych Elm Project piece Caroline contrasts commonplace and more valuable materials, adopting traditional casting techniques to inlay precious metal into the grain of the wood, mirroring the wings of the white-letter hairstreak butterfly which breeds on the tree. She explains: "By contrasting these materials, I hope to express the ecological value of the elm to be surpassing the cost of the materials and the luxury of jewellery as a whole".

Images:
Necklace: RBGE/Lynsey Wilson,
other images: RBGE/Amy Copeman.

Ulmus glabra ssp. montana

'Son of Wych' 02/11 20/08
in the
Chinese Hillside,
R-E-B-G
(Self-seeded?)

full of right-angles!
(one leaf to its neighbour)

barely attached
yellow green, scuse of flying
leaves

only little children notice me through the gap in the bamboo

Kate Downie

Kate is best known for her paintings of urban and industrial landscapes but has always harboured a passion for trees. Whilst living in Amsterdam in the 1980s she encountered trees immortalised in magnificent works by Van Gogh, Mondrian and Keifer, increasing her passion – she is now forever drawn to particular trees and feels compelled to try to understand some of their growth forms through drawing. "Making these drawings", she says, "keeps me rooted in what is otherwise a very strange world".

This is evident in her limited edition screen print of the Garden's wych elm – based on a drawing – which she made in 1994, as part of a project to light up the windows of the Edinburgh City Council offices on George IV Bridge (see Chapter 9). Sadly, this single drawing is all that seems to have survived from the project. Kate writes: "Alas, little remains of those studies and designs now, as, ephemeral as a stage set, all was struck once the show was over and the children are long gone. Even the building is gone. There is nothing so invisible as the recent past".

Like others she remembers being drawn to the tree, a lone native "among a forest of immigrants". Standing in a boggy patch "over 200 years old and bearing the scars of lopped branches and extravagant growth, to me it wore an air of rough Scottish naturalism

amongst the exotica of the humanly acquired and nurtured arboretum". Fourteen years later, inspired by the Wych Elm Project, she returned to the area to draw wild seedlings, direct descendants of the original tree, that had established themselves among the bramble and bamboo of the Chinese Hillside. Although these are still small trees, Kate already recognises "the genetic imprint of the great Mother tree, the dominant branches side sweeping and tumbling westward in a very familiar way".

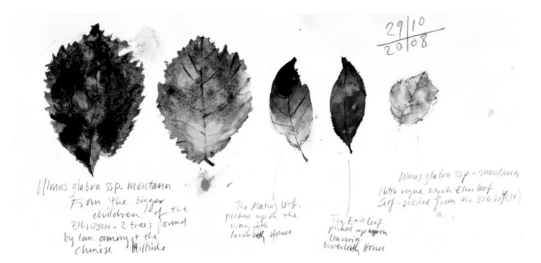

Images: Michael Wolchover.

Rob Elliot

Rob is a sawmiller's son and has been surrounded by wood all his life. Rob produces furniture that is distinctive and often quirky, from fairytale beds in burr-elm to stunning rocking chairs. He has specialised in elm, especially wych elm, which he admires for its interesting grain and colouring. He sources all of his timber from dead trees and is proud of the fact that he is able to bring out the hidden beauty of the timber without harming the environment from which the trees originate. The mirror and hall table that Rob has contributed to the Wych Elm Project were designed by David and Catherine Buxton who commissioned the pieces. They were keen to be part of the Project and even visited the Cousland sawmill in the early stages to see the boards in their raw form. David writes: "The finished pieces were every bit as good as we had imagined, with the quality of craftsmanship second to none. You cannot truly foresee the outcome of a project in timber such as elm because the markings do not speak for themselves until the final finish is applied but the way that Rob selected the timber to show off the grain of the wood to its best advantage is an indication of his many years of skilled work with this particular Scottish tree. One special surprise was the beauty of the grain in the base of the drawer that remains hidden until it is opened". Rob adds: "Although the design was pretty much all the client, the construction techniques are mine. The corner finger-joints were taken from my 'Yin Yang' tables".

Images:
Unfinished piece: Rob Elliot,
other images: RBGE/Amy Copeman.

Images:
Main: RBGE/Lynsey Wilson,
inset: RBGE/Amy Copeman.

Mette Fruergaard-Jensen

Mette is Danish and trained in pottery at the Arts and Crafts School in Copenhagen. She had her own pottery workshop for 25 years, and spent two years in Tanzania teaching young people pottery, before retraining in wood and metal work. Since 1996 she has specialised in making boxes using natural materials such as wood, copper, amber, bone and horn. Most of her materials are recycled and found on the beach, woodpile or scrapyard.

Since 2000 she has lived and worked in Scotland. Her boxes have been on show in exhibitions and art fairs, and she was among an international group of designer-makers whose work was included in the touring exhibition and book *Celebrating Boxes*. She was also a contributor to the *Gifted* exhibition at the National Museum of Scotland in 2007, and her work appears in the book *400 Wooden Boxes*.

Mette enjoys combining different materials that complement each other. For her Wych Elm Project piece she has combined copper,

a sensitive material that reacts to different treatments such as heat, acid and polishing, with the wood of the wych elm. She describes how both materials share a softness and a golden glow.

Images: RBGE/Amy Copeman.

Ian Grant

Ian, from Fochabers, has developed a unique form of inlay, cut from bundles of contrasting hardwood, that is reminiscent of both Scottish tweed and tartan and has inspired his company name 'Tartan from Trees'. Edinburgh's National Museum of Scotland has acquired one of his tartan 'button inlay' tables and three of his marquetry cubes for their 20th-century collection; Ian also designed and made the Millennium table for Duff House in Banff. Ian's 'antelope table' for the Wych Elm Project is one of a series of animal pieces he has made. It incorporates his hallmark tartan button detailing where the legs penetrate the upper surface. The effect is striking both to the eye and to the touch, as the harder woods stand proud, producing a textured surface the fingers can appreciate.

The client, Mrs Shepherd, had commissioned works from Ian previously and as a frequent visitor to the Edinburgh Garden was keen that she and Ian should be part of the Wych Elm Project. The antelope console incorporates an elm burr from Mrs Shepherd's Morayshire garden as the belly of the remarkably animal-like table. Ian describes how it hangs like a "giant polished pebble ... a rich, dark

contrast to the pale, swirly, wych elm grain". Instead of cursing the slightly undulating boards that he was supplied with, Ian enjoyed incorporating a more sculptural feel into the beast, with muscular legs and highly strokable surfaces. As Mrs Shepherd muses, "it looks like it has just walked into the room from the garden outside".

Images: Ian Grant.

Roger Hall

Roger has a background in woodworking, furniture making and design but more recently has shifted his focus to letter-carving, an interest developed during a period of architectural work and stimulated by seeing Richard Kindersley's work in the Museum of Scotland in Edinburgh. The Scottish Lettercutters Association, of which Roger is a member, has also been an important influence on his work. Most of the Association's members work in stone but Roger works exclusively in hardwood, sometimes creating various effects by ebonising, charring or painting the wood. In the Wych Elm Project piece for Professor Iain Ledingham, Roger has chosen to leave part of the surface in its grey, weathered form, circling the letters around the central organic shape. Professor Ledingham enjoys woodworking himself and took an active part, along with Roger's mentor Martin Wenham, in selecting the design for the lettering. The inscription 'he who has planted a tree has not passed in vain upon the earth' (a translation via French from the Arabic original) was Iain Ledingham's choice.

To develop his calligraphy skills Roger has attended classes at Edinburgh College of Art. His studies and work in letter-carving have led to an appreciation of poetry and a playfulness with words. For his second piece 'another day', inspired by work of Glasgow poet Larry Butler,

Roger has collaborated with Susie Leiper, a distinguished calligrapher. Together they have created a new typeface, which is both bold and naturalistic, perfectly suited to the large, elegantly grained boards.

Roger works in a studio surrounded by a bewildering variety of hand tools, many acquired second-hand, that he lovingly cares for with oil and stone. The razor-sharpness of his chisels and gauges plus the fact that Roger's accomplished cello playing requires his fingers to be in pristine condition explains the glove on his left hand when he is at his work bench!

Images: RBGE/Amy Copeman.

Michaela Huber

Michaela trained as a cabinet maker in her home town of München before coming to Scotland in 1980. She worked for Ben Dawson, the Musselburgh-based furniture makers who created the furniture for the John Hope Gateway café, and in 1986 set up her own business. Michaela has a reputation for excellent craftsmanship and a confidence which is evident in the quality of her work and her relationship with her clients.

Most of Michaela's pieces result from commissions, and the bookcase she made for the Wych Elm Project was no exception. The client was Paul Broda, a former Trustee of the Royal Botanic Garden Edinburgh, who designed the piece for housing part of his library within his Edinburgh New Town flat. Michaela is enthusiastic about converting the ideas and feelings of her clients about their environment into the beauty of the piece she creates. Her workshop is well equipped with modern machinery, but the subtle curves in the wych elm bookcase required careful hand-finishing. The piece exhibits some of the green streaks characteristic of wych elm wood, which tend to develop a slight bloom after oil-finishing (see Chapter 4).

Images: RBGE/Amy Copeman.

Geoff King

Geoff began his career making toys, for which he received many awards. He later moved on to joinery, furniture making and writing for *The Woodworker* magazine, as well as renovating an old croft house near Tain, Ross-shire, where he now lives with his wife, son, cat and hens. Following an illness, and during a period of convalescence, he took up wooden jewellery making.

Geoff's designs are cut with a fretsaw and knives from a range of woods. He is a hoarder of off-cuts and odd bits of wood, revelling in their textures, grains and colours. His materials include reclaimed timber from a Swedish shipwreck and bog oak from the Somerset fens, as well as semi-precious stones like turquoise and amber. Geoff's influences include Pictish and Celtic designs, Art Nouveau, the natural world and British mythological figures like the Green Man.

The owl bangle he contributed to the Wych Elm Project was a challenge to make because the multi-directional grain of the wood does not lend itself to fine work of this kind. Geoff had to be painstakingly careful and work very slowly to avoid digging into and ripping the grain. However, the grain pattern and colour was well suited to capturing the markings on the owl's wing, and the interlocking nature of the grain gives strength to the piece.

Images: RBGE/Amy Copeman.

Beth Legg

Beth comes from Caithness, and her work is inspired by the vast open spaces of the north of Scotland, together with her collection of found objects. She trained in art and design at Edinburgh College of Art, and while specialising in jewellery she is part of the movement that is breaking down traditional boundaries in this field. She is a keen observer and has likened her work bench to a laboratory where she "works intuitively with her materials rather than contriving designs". She is conscious of the embedded memory within her materials and the way in which they have been "touched by different eroding processes which give them resonance and a sense of preciousness". She believes that the opportunity to work with pieces of 200-year-old wych elm is very relevant to her making ethos and is a rare chance to work closely with a unique material that has a real sense of history engrained within it.

Beth's piece for the Wych Elm Project is a necklace in which she has set the unique wood in the way that traditional jewellers would a precious stone. During the research for a project she likes to draw and take photographs, and she visited the Edinburgh Garden to investigate the landscape and context where the wych elm was growing.

Images:
Necklace: Beth Legg,
other images: RBGE/Amy Copeman.

Susie Leiper

Susie worked for many years as a freelance book editor, specialising in books on Chinese art and archaeology. She learnt her calligraphy skills first in Hong Kong under Derek Pao, and then at evening classes at Edinburgh College of Art. Having studied in both Hong Kong and Scotland she feels that "Western calligraphy needs a voice: it deserves the artistic status that calligraphy has for so long held in the East". Her traditional 'quills on vellum' calligraphy includes three years as a scribe on Donald Jackson's *St John's Bible*, the first handwritten bible for 500 years, and more recently a 2,500-word commemorative charter for the 400th anniversary of the Middle Temple in London. Her work also encompasses more innovative styles including pointed brush lettering and painting on Chinese paper, and handmade artists' books inspired by her love of all things Chinese. She has exhibited widely including in the National Museum of Scotland and the Royal Scottish Academy in Edinburgh and the V&A in London, and is a Fellow of the Society of Scribes and Illuminators.

Susie collaborated with Roger Hall, designing the lettering for their piece 'another day'. Her own contribution to the Wych Elm Project involves hand-painted lettering on two matching pieces of elm prepared by Roger. She has chosen a poem by Valerie Gillies written during her involvement in the Wych Elm Project community projects (see Chapter 9). With her Chinese connections, and because the wych elm grew originally near the Chinese Hillside in the Edinburgh Garden, Susie hopes the piece will resonate in some way with China.

Image:
Portrait: RBGE/Amy Copeman.

Neil Martin

Neil studied fine art and design, and then proceeded to train as a furniture maker under the guidance of cabinet maker Nick Goodall. Although Neil still makes handmade furniture to commission, he is probably best known for his 'vessels' – individual sculptural pieces made from Scottish hardwoods. For the past six years he has also worked part-time as a Ranger at the Royal Botanic Garden Edinburgh, surrounded by the Garden's diverse collection of trees from all over the world. However, for his sculpture and furniture Neil uses almost exclusively Scottish native trees, which he sources locally. He finds the history of the timber interesting, as do many of his clients.

Neil finds Scottish hardwoods an ideal medium for sculpting organic forms. "A piece of timber might have a particular idiosyncrasy that captures your imagination", says Neil. The process is intuitive: "I just begin by stripping the wood until I feel enough of the wood is exposed". With his training in both fine art and furniture making, Neil views this as being in direct contrast to the methods of a painter who generally adds layers of paint until satisfied. Like many of the emerging woodworkers,

Neil does not think a mark or knot in the wood is a defect but rather something that can be brought into the character of the piece. "I try not to change too much of what nature has created, instead focusing on the inherent beauty of the wood and giving it a second life through my work."

Images:
Wood block: Neil Martin,
finished vessel: RBGE/Lynsey Wilson,
other images: RBGE/Amy Copeman.

Mark Norris

Mark is one of Britain's leading designers and makers of hand-built harps. He originally trained in harpsichord making with Arnold Dolmetsch Ltd before returning to Scotland to set up a harp-making workshop in the Old School at Stobo in the Scottish Borders. Over the last 27 years, Mark's harps have achieved an international reputation for innovative design, fine craftsmanship and outstanding musical quality, and his instruments are used by many respected performers and recording artists in Scotland and around the world. He is married to the composer and harp virtuoso Savourna Stevenson, who was a leading contributor to the community projects that formed part of the Wych Elm Project (see Chapter 9).

Mark had never used wych elm as a material for his harps before, but was interested in the challenge that it presented. For the Wych Elm Project he was particularly keen to make his first Aeolian harp (a harp to be played by the wind), and felt this would be an appropriate way to utilise the decorative grain and other qualities of the wych elm timber.

At the time of writing Mark had not begun construction but was testing design ideas and working on a prototype for the harp, which has

been commissioned by Gordon and Ena Baxter for the Community Garden overlooking the River Spey at Fochabers, original home of the Baxters' highly successful food manufacturing business. Gordon, now retired from the family firm, and his wife have been helping to regenerate the area, with some assistance from the Royal Botanic Garden Edinburgh in creating a new garden. Mark, generally known for his small, 34-string Norris harps, plans to construct a slightly larger 39-string design with extra-long bass strings which will respond well to the wind. The harp will use metal rather than gut strings.

To ensure the harp's survival outside in the Scottish climate, the commission includes a specially designed open-sided, glass-roofed pavilion, also to be constructed of wych elm timber. This commission thus provides an unusual combination of musical instrument and architectural design, both constructed using wych elm. Mark hopes to create a mechanism enabling the harp to revolve within the pavilion, producing different musical sounds as the strings respond to the changing direction of the wind. In classical mythology, the north, south, east and west winds (Boreus, Notus, Eurus and Zephyrus) were under the rule of Aeolus. Along with the sailors, the kite-fliers, and now the wind-power generators, Mark will be hoping to please Aeolus and attract some fine, brisk winds in Edinburgh and Fochabers to play the new harp.

Images:
Pavilion sketch: Mark Norris, meeting with Baxters: RBGE/Mairi Gillies, portrait: RBGE/Amy Copeman.

Angus Ross

Angus works surrounded by woodworking machines and is proud of the fact that his workshop in Aberfeldy, Perthshire, has been used for woodworking continuously since 1870. Angus works mainly to commission and his background in industrial product design means he begins with a thorough investigation into who the piece is for, and where, when, how and why it will be used. His avowed aim is to create a piece that "will bring pleasure in its use, is beautiful but unpretentious and may contain an element of surprise".

Marion Dunlop, the client for his coffee table has a great fondness for the Royal Botanic Garden Edinburgh and can well remember pushing a pram around the Garden and picnicking near the wych elm. She was delighted with the idea of owning part of such a memorable tree and wanted a small table that would complement the frame rocking chair that was a previous commission from Angus.

The table uses a similar section to the chair and employs the same idea of linked frames.

The concept for Angus's second piece, the Collector's Chair, was far from simple. A circular drawer for the storage and presentation of collectable objects, free to rotate within a circular chair, was a difficult brief for a commission. Angus's solution to this challenge was to build the chair up from small sections of wood, reserving the pieces with the most beautiful grain and colouring for the sculpted top rail. The client, Steve Swan, has a passion for Japanese design, and inspiration for the piece came from traditional Japanese storage boxes and chests (called *tansu*) as well as intricate Japanese joint-work. Angus explains: "The idea of the Collector's Chair stemmed from my interest in the way people use and interact with things, how they collect and present objects... and the unexpected!"

Images: RBGE/Amy Copeman.

David Swift

David is an artist and toymaker, and has had many years of experience working with children (including those with autism). His toys are probably not, however, the sort you would want to give every boisterous ten-year-old. Some have been described as 'surreal', and he has been influenced by both the circus (he once trained as a clown) and puppetry. David explains: "I employ the visual language of toys because it is direct, colourful and accessible, but use it to say (hopefully) some subtle or complex things about life, love and everything". He loves to travel and is particularly drawn to Japan – where he was recently a resident artist at the Arima Toys and Automata Museum – and to Italy, where he now lives.

In 2004, David was the recipient of a prestigious Creative Scotland award from the Scottish Arts Council to animate some of his toys. He chose to collaborate with animator Jonathan Charles to make a short film, *Nocture in Sea Shark*, described as a tale of love, betrayal and ice-cream, which is set in Sicily and Orkney and based on a fragment from the medieval Italian epic *Orlando Furioso*.

David's toy boat 'Wychcraft' has a keel from the Garden's wych elm but also incorporates pieces of wood from two of Edinburgh's twin towns – yew from Kyoto and cherry from near Florence. The nautical theme is highly appropriate as wych elm was – and still is – important for wooden boat-building (see Chapter 4). His tiny vessel reflects his passion for the miniature as well as the immense pleasure he derives from concocting cross-cultural mixtures. David cites among the influences for this piece the Japanese belief in 'fox wedding weather' and Akira Kurosawa's film *Dreams*. "I liked the idea of telling secrets to trees," he adds, "so this mysterious boat carries an intriguing cargo – a bit like a message in a bottle...". The piece has been acquired by the Arima Toys Museum in Kobe, Japan.

Images: Andrea Barghi.

Jennifer Watt

Jennifer works in many materials, but is best known for her work in wood. Jennifer's current fascination is with "birth in its many forms, whether it is a chestnut opening to reveal its glossy inner shell, a seedling pushing through the ground or the birth of a baby". She describes how in her New Beginnings project she is trying to replicate not just the smooth sensual shapes but also the feelings birth evokes. In her more figurative pieces she also explores the bond between mother and child and the tenderness that exists between them.

Jennifer's most recent explorations of birth harmonise with a theme that runs throughout the Wych Elm Project – the cycle of life, death and rebirth. She describes how wych elm is particularly suited to her work as her sculpture is "nearly always very simple in form so the colour and markings of the elm are shown to their best on the simple shapes". The relatively small pieces of wood that were available to her created a challenge, but her use of dark wood in the centre creates a successful contrast with the wych elm. The simple, smooth surfaces of the pods show the rich markings of the grain to perfection, the patterns becoming part of the sculpture, echoing its contours and form.

Images:
Sculpture: Mike Rothnie,
other images: RBGE/Amy Copeman.

'Wychcraft' by David Swift.
Image: Andrea Barghi.

Contact details

Contact details

Nigel Bridges
Phone 01835 822818
Email bridgesnig@aol.com
Web www.nigelbridges.com

Isabell Buenz
Phone 07751 649161
Email isabuenz@hotmail.com
Web www.isabellbuenz.co.uk

Chris Butler
Phone 01450 870786
Email chris@christopherbutlerfurniture.com
Web www.christopherbutlerfurniture.com

Fiona Campbell
Phone 07899 998832
Email mail@fionacampbellfurniture.co.uk
Web www.fionacampbellfurniture.co.uk

Sam Chinnery
Phone 07831 366603
Email sam@samchinnery.co.uk
Web www.samchinnery.co.uk

Caroline Cloughley
Phone 07851 283718
Email ccloughley1@hotmail.com

Kate Downie
Phone 0131 476 7028
Email kate@katedownie.com
Web www.katedownie.com

Rob Elliot
Phone 01750 22243
Email rob.elliot@ic24.net
Web www.robelliotfurniture.com

Mette Fruergaard-Jensen
Phone 0131 476 4645
Email mettefruergaard@hotmail.com

Ian Grant
Phone 01343 880204

Roger Hall
Phone 0131 447 0050
Email roger-hall@tiscali.co.uk

Michaela Huber
Phone 0131 660 9534
Email Michaela.huber57@googlemail.com
Web www.michaela-huber.co.uk

Harry Jamieson
Phone 01479 821676
Email harry@clanrods.com
Web www.clanrods.com

Jane Kelly
Phone 01968 677854
Email Jane.Kelly2@virgin.net

Geoff King
Phone 01862 871639
Email info@woodlandtreasures.co.uk
Web www.woodlandtreasures.co.uk

Beth Legg
Phone 07810 273455
Email bfaraway@hotmail.com
Web www.bethlegg.com

Susie Leiper
Phone 0131 558 1405
Email susieleiper@hotmail.com

Neil Martin
Phone 0131 663 5388
Email contactme@neilmartin.biz
Web www.neilmartin.biz

Mark Norris
Phone 01721 760298
Email norris.harps@virgin.net
Web www.norrisharps.com

Angus Ross
Phone 01887 829857
Email angus@angusross.co.uk
Web www.angusross.co.uk

David Swift
Phone 00 39 0575 532010
Email swiftcurran@hotmail.com

Jennifer Watt
Phone 01848 331524
Email nowwatt@lineone.net
Web www.jenniferwatt.co.uk

Autumn wych elm leaves.
Image: RBGE/Max Coleman.

Biographies

Biographies

Mary Beith

Mary Beith is an author and journalist with a particular interest in the social history, archaeology and traditional remedies of the Highlands and Islands. She has written a fortnightly column, *Deanamh a' Leighis* ('Making the Cure'), in the West Highland Free Press since 1989 and her *Healing Threads: Traditional medicines of the Highlands and Islands* was published in 1995. She has given many talks on the subject throughout Scotland. Her most recent book (2008) is *An t-Ubhal Seunta* ('The Magic Apple'), an illustrated story for children. She lives on the north coast of Sutherland where she enjoys pottering in her garden.

Image: Tom Baker Photography.

Max Coleman

Max Coleman was born in London and remembers the loss of elms during the 1970s. An interest in trees from an early age led to the study of Botany. He obtained his first degree from the University of Bristol. After a period of work in nature conservation, he gained an MSc from the University of Edinburgh, which included a research project on the British elms. Max has published research on elms and is the referee for *Ulmus* for the Botanical Society of the British Isles. Max works at the Royal Botanic Garden Edinburgh interpreting botanical science for the public.

Brian Coppins

Brian Coppins has studied lichens for 44 years. For the last 35 years he has been the Lichen and Ascomycete Taxonomist at the Royal Botanic Garden Edinburgh. Geographically, his interests have mainly concerned the British Isles and western Europe, but he has been on expeditions to the Far East, Borneo and Chile. Brian has co-authored *The Lichen Flora of Great Britain and Ireland* and produced numerous reports for government agencies and NGOs relating to biodiversity survey and monitoring. Brian is a past president of the British Lichen Society, and recipient of that society's Ursula Duncan Award in recognition of his contributions to lichenology.

Ian Edwards

Ian Edwards began his career as a woodland ecologist and has a lifetime interest in wood and woodcraft. He has worked at the Royal Botanic Garden Edinburgh for 25 years and is currently responsible for exhibitions and events. He has worked previously as a forestry officer in Malawi and as education officer at Brisbane Botanic Garden. Ian received a Winston Churchill Fellowship to investigate the role of volunteers in education in the USA and Canada. It was through his effort that the Garden's wych elm was saved and the Wych Elm Project was born. He is also director of Reforesting Scotland, a charity dedicated to restoring native forest and a woodland culture to Scotland.

Stephan Helfer

Stephan Helfer was born in Southern Germany when elms were still plentiful in that part of Europe. He gained his first degree at the University of Tübingen, where he specialised in a group of fungal pathogens called the rusts. After post-doctoral work in Aberdeen, Stephan took up a post as Electron Microscopist/Mycologist at the Royal Botanic Garden Edinburgh. This developed into full-time mycology with a remit to investigate pathogenic micro-fungi, such as rusts, mildews, smuts and wilt pathogens such as the Dutch elm disease fungus. His current work is split between research on European rusts and advisory and research work on pathogens of garden ornamentals.

Peter Toaig

Peter Toaig was born in Marske-by-the-Sea in northeast England. After gaining a mathematics degree at the University of Manchester he studied furniture design and construction at Manchester College of Art and Technology. In 1998 Peter and Garry Olson organised the project *One Tree*, an attempt to make the best possible use of a single English oak. The result was a national touring exhibition and a book featuring work by 75 artists, designers and makers. Peter currently has workshops in Stirling and Cumbria. He has served as a Specialist Advisor to the Scottish Arts Council and as chairman of the Scottish Furniture Makers Association.

Roy Watling

Roy Watling, until retirement, was Senior Principal Scientific Officer and Head of Mycology and Plant Pathology at the Royal Botanic Garden Edinburgh. He graduated with a BSc from the University of Sheffield before gaining a PhD from the University of Edinburgh and DSc from his former alma mater. He was awarded the MBE by Her Majesty the Queen in 1996 and is a Fellow of the Royal Society of Edinburgh, from whom he received the Patrick Neill Medal for Excellence in Natural Sciences. He has been a committee member or fellow of many mycological and learned societies. He has maintained links with the mycological work of the Royal Botanic Garden Edinburgh and continues to communicate his passion for fungi.

Autumn tints in a wych elm
overhanging a burn.
Image: RBGE/Max Coleman.

Index

Index

Note: Page numbers in italics refer to photographs and illustrations.

'Achievement Tree' *77, 80, 83, 83*
Acrocordia gemmata 54
'After the Elm' 73
Age of the tree 12
Agonimia 52; *A. allobata* 54
Agrocybe cylindracea 57
Ainu people 47
'Alan Mitchell's
Trees of Britain' 12
Alasdair of Glengarry 32-3
Alternative medicines 38
Alva Primary School,
Clackmannanshire 80, 84, *84*
Amandinea punctata 51
Anaptychia ciliaris 53, 54
Ancient Tree Hunt 76
Animal fodder 14, 26, 48
Anthostoma melanotes 61
Arbuscular endomycorrhiza 58
Argyll 68, 76
Armillaria 65; *A. bulbosa* 58;
A. mellea 58
Arrow manufacture 15, 42
Artists
    Bridges, Nigel 88-9
    Buenz, Isabell 90-1
    Butler, Chris 92-3
    Campbell, Fiona 94-5
    Chinnery, Sam 96-7
    Cloughley, Caroline 98-9
    Contact details 134
    Downie, Kate 78-9, 100-1
    Elliot, Rob 47, 102-3
    Fruergaard-Jensen, Mette 104-5
    Grant, Ian 106-7
    Hall, Roger 108-9
    Holmes, Chris 78, 80, 83, 87
    Huber, Michaela 110-1
    Introduction 14, 85-7
    Jamieson, Harry 112-3
    Kelly, Jane 114-5
    King, Geoff 116-7
    Legg, Beth 118-9
    Leiper, Susie 120-1
    Martin, Neil 122-3
    Norris, Mark 124-5
    Ross, Angus 126-7
    Stead, Tim 14, *46*, 87
    Swift, David 128-9
    Watt, Jennifer 130-1
Athelopsis lembospora 59
Atinian elm 35
'Atlas of the British Flora, The' 73

Bacidia 52; *B. circumspecta* 53, 54;
B. incompta 51, 53, 54; *B. rubella* 54;
B. subincompta 53; *B. vermifera* 53
Bagpipes *45*
Ballachulish, Highland *2*
Bark 16-7, *48*, 48, 50, *68*
    healing qualities 37
    medicinal uses 47
Beetles
    Dutch elm disease 17, 26, 67-8,
    67, 68, 74-5
Beith, Mary 136
Benmore Botanic Garden 68
Berriedale, Highland *19*
Beth-Luis-Nuin 31
Biatora epixanthoides 52;
B. sphaeroides 52
Biatoridium 52; *B. delitescens* 53;
B. monasteriensis 53
Bibliography 140-1
Biographies 136-7
Biological control measures
    Dutch elm disease 70
Biological species concept 23
Bjerkandera adusta 59
Boat making 14, 45
    Cornish pilot gig *39*, 44-5, *44*
'Botanic Ash' exhibition 13
Bow making 31, 40-1
Bowls 45
Brahadail 31
Brahan Elm *29, 74*
Brahan Estate, Easter Ross *29*
Bridges, Nigel 88-9, 134
Brighton 67
British Lichen Society 54
Bryophytes 52
Buenz, Isabell 90-1, 134
Burr-wood 66
Bute 68, 76
Butler, Chris 92-3, 134
Butterflies 16

'Cad Goddeu' 34
Calocera cornea 60
Caloplaca flavorubescens 53;
C. luteoalba 16, 50-1, *51*, 53, 54;
C. ulcerosa 54
Campbell, Fiona 94-5, 134
Camperdown House, Dundee 24
'Camperdownii' *23*, 24

Candelariella 51
Cankers 66
Carlops, Scottish Borders *15*, 22
Carmichael, Alexander 30, 33
'Carmina Gadelica' 33
Cartwheel manufacture 43-4
Castle Esplanade, Edinburgh 32
Cattle feed 14, 26, 48
Celtic Rainforest zone 53
Ceriporia reticulata 59
Chaenotheca brachypoda 53;
C. chlorella 53-4; *C. gracilenta* 53;
C. hispidula 53; *C. laevigata* 53;
C. trichialis 53
Chairs 44-5, *45, 47*
Characteristics of elm 14
Chemicals 65
China 48
Chinnery, Sam 96-7, 134
Chondrostereum purpureum 58
Clare, John 35-6
Climatic conditions 64-5
Clissett, Philip 47
Clitopilus hobsonii 60
Cloughley, Caroline 98-9, 134
Coffins 43-4
Coleman, Max *78*, 136
Collema 52; *C. fasciculare* 53, 54;
C. fragrans 53; *C. nigrescens* 53;
C. occultatum 53, 54
Commemorative elms 35
Community projects 77-84
Conservation Foundation 72, 76
Coppins, Brian 136
Coprinellus disseminatus 58
Cordage 47-8
Cornish pilot gig *39*, 44-5, *44*
Cowdenburn, Scottish Borders 33
Craftspeople, *see* Artists
Crepidotus cesatii 60; *C. mollis* 60
Crewe Toll, Midlothian 44
Cryptosporella hypodermia 61
Cucurbitaria naucosa 62
Cultivars of wych elm
    'Camperdownii' *23*, 24
    'Exoniensis' 24
    'Horizontalis' 24, *30*
    'Lutescens' 24
    'Nana' *23*, 24, *71*

Cuttings 75-6, *72, 76*
Cyanolichens 52
Cyathus striatus 60-1, *60*
Cylindrobasidium evolvens 59

Daedalea quercina 59
Dasyscyphus 61
Datronia mollis 59
Deakin, Roger 18
Dedications 35
Degelia 52
Denmark 40
'd-factors' 70
Dimerella lutea 52, *53*
Diplodia melaena* 62
Diplotomma alboatrum 51
Disease, Dutch elm,
    see Dutch elm disease
Diversification 70
DNA fingerprinting 22
Dothiorella sarmentorum 65
Downie, Kate 78-9, 100-1, 134
'Drawings of British Plants' 12
Driftwood 44
Drought 64
Dunskey Estate, Dumfries
    and Galloway 75
Dutch elm disease 12-4, 17, 26, 28,
45, 56, 63-70, *63, 64, 65, 66, 67*
    efforts to counter 17-8, 69-70
    impact 67-8, *67, 72*
    recovery 70-6
Dutch Elm Disease
(Local Authorities) Order 1984 67

Edinburgh *32, 42*, 65, *74*, 76
Edlin, Herbert 42
Edwards, Ian 137
Elliot, Rob 47, 102-3, 134
Ellis, Martin and Pamela 62
'Elm' 15, 34
'Elm Decline' 17, 25-6
Elm Map project 75-6
Encoelia siparia 62
'Englishman's Flora, The' 35, 40
Environmental conditions 20-1,
24-8, 64-5
'Epitaph for the Elm' 73
Ercol 46
Erysiphe clandestina 66

Eutypella **61**; *E. stellulata* **61**

Evernia prunastri **52**

Exeter **24**

Exhibitions
  'Botanic Ash' 1993 **13**
  'One Tree' 2001 **13**
  planning **13**
  'With the Grain' **46**

Exidia thuretiana **60**

Exidiopsis calcea **60**

'Exoniensis' **24**

Farm implements **42**

Felling **12-3, 67**

Field resistance **74**

Fife **76**

Flagelloscypha citrispora **60**

Flammulina velutipes **55, 57**

Flodden campaign 1513 **41**

'Flora Celtica' **45, 47**

'Flora Scotica' **47**

Flowers **24**

Foliar pathogens **66**

Folklore **14-5, 30-8**

Food supplement **48**

Forestry Commission **13**

Forestry Commission Scotland
75, 80, 144

Forrest, Julie **84**

Forster, E.M. **38**

Fossil evidence **17, 21, 26, 73**

France **18**

Fruergaard-Jensen, Mette **104-5, 134**

Fruit *2, 27, 48*

Fuel **47**

Fungi **15-6, 55-62, 65**
  Dutch elm disease,
    see Dutch elm disease

Fungicides **69, 70**

Furniture **45-6**

Furniture makers, *see* Artists

Fuscopannaria **52**; *F. ignobilis* **53**;
F. sampaiana **53**

Galerina unicolor **60**

Gallows **34-5**, *34*

Ganoderma **58**; *G. applanatum* **58**;
G. australe **58**

Gerard *21, 37, 42, 48*

Gibbet Tree **34**

Gillies, Valerie **10, 81-2**, *82*

Gilpin, William **12, 20**

Glen Lochay, Loch Tay,
Perthshire *20*

Gomphillus calycioides **53**

Gough, Toby *11*

Graddon, W.D. **61**

Grain structure **14**, *14*, **44-5**

Grant, Ian *85*, **106-7, 134**

Grant, Miranda **80**

Grieve, Kenny **80, 83-4**

Grieve, Mrs **48**

Grigson, Geoffrey **35, 40**

Grove **62**

Growth rings **12**

Gyalecta **52**; *G. flotowii* **53, 54**;
G. ulmi *50, 50*, **53**

Habrostictis rubra **62**

Haddington, Earl of **42**

Hall, Roger **108-9, 134**

Hampstead Heath, London **35**

Hapalopilus nidulans **59**

Hardwood cuttings **75-6**, *72, 76*

Healing qualities **36-7**

Healing rites **36**

Helfer, Stephan **137**

Henningsomyces candidus **60**

Heterodermia obscurata **53**

Hirneola auricula **59, 60**

'History of Herbal Plants, A' **35**

Hogarth, William *34*

Holmes, Chris **78, 80, 83, 87**, *87*

Homer **43, 64**

'Horizontalis' **24**, *30*

'Howards End' **38**

Huber, Michaela **110-1, 134**

Hudson, William **21**

Huntingtowerfield Bleach
and Dyeworks, Almondbank,
Perthshire **42**

Hybrid swarms **23**

Hyperphyscia **51**

Hyphodontia pruni **59**

Hypholoma fasciculare **58**

Hypsizygus tessulatus **57**;
H. ulmarius **57**

Ice Ages **24, 62**

Identification **21-5**

'Idle Prentice Executed at
Tyburn, The' *34*

'Iliad' **64**

Imported wood **69**

'In Memoriam' **32**

Insecticides **70**

Inverleith Park, Edinburgh *65*

Inverness **68, 74**

Irish Brehon Law **32**

Italy **18**

Jamieson, Harry **112-3, 134**

Japan **47**

Jeffries, Richard **35**

Jewel and Esk College **82**

Johnson, Thomas **41**

Kaimes School, Edinburgh **77, 78,
80, 83**, *83*

Keats, John **30**

Kelly, Jane **114-5, 134**

King, Geoff **116-7, 134**

Kintyre **57**

Kipling, Rudyard **35, 43**

Kirkby, Sharon **80, 83**

Kretzschmaria **58**

Kyrgyzstan **81**

Lachnum deflexum **61-2**

'Lady of the Lake, The' **32, 36**

Lake District **73**

Latheronwheel, Highland **25**

Lauder, Sir Thomas Dick **12**

Le Strange, Richard **35**

Leadhills, Lanarkshire **45**

Leaves **48, 66**

Lecania chlorotiza **52**

Lecanora carpinea **52**; *L. chlarotera* **51**;
L. horiza **53, 54**; *L. persimilis* **52**

Lecidella elaeochroma **52**

Legg, Beth **118-9, 134**

Leiper, Susie **120-1, 134**

Leptogium **52**; *L. brebissonii* **53**;
L. cochleatum **53**; *L. hibernicum* **53**;
L. saturninum **53**

Lichens **15-7, 49, 50-4**
  British Lichen Society **54**
  Red Data Book categories **53**
  Xanthorion community **17, 51**

Lightfoot **47**

Limus Norlandicus **62**

Linnaeus **21**

Livingston Mill **42**

Lobaria **52**; *L. pulmonaria* **52**

Local Biodiversity Action Plans **76**

Longbows **40-1**

Lopadostoma gastrinum **61**

Lord Ancrum's Wood,
Dalkeith, Midlothian **80**

Lothian Trees and Timber
Sawmill, Cousland **45, 79**, *86*

'Lutescens' **24**

Lyomyces sambuci **59**

Maggio, Bonnie **84**

Mainland, Orkney Islands *138*

Martin, Neil **122-3, 134**

McTavish, Roddy **80**

Mears, Ray **48**

Medicinal uses **37-8, 47-8**

Megalocystidium luridum **59**

Melanelixia subaurifera **51**

Melanohalea exasperata **52**, *52*;
M. exasperatula **52**

Melville, Ronald **22**

'Microfungi on Land Plants' **62**

Microscopic fungi **58**

Millard, Paul *80-1*

Millmore, near Killin,
Stirlingshire **36**

Milton **36**

Moldova **66**

Monocultures **70**

Morchella esculenta **61**

Mull **15, 31, 42**

Mull of Galloway **73**

Mushrooms, *see* Fungi

Mycena **60**; *M. adscendens* **60**;
M. meliigena **60**; *M. pseudocorticola* **60**

'Nana' *23, 24, 71*

Nancarrow, Andrew **39, 45**

'National Vegetation
Classification' **27**

Native Woodlands Survey
of Scotland **75**

Nectria **66**; *N. cinnabarina* **61**, *61*, **66**

Nephroma **52**

Netherlands **18**
'New Atlas of the British
and Irish Flora' **73**
New Zealand **69**
Newbattle Abbey College **80-1**
Nicolson, Alexander **33-4**
Norris, Mark **124-5, 134**
North America **44, 66-7, 69**
Norway **26**

Ogham Tree Alphabet **15, 31-2**
Old Irish tree lists **32**
'One Tree' exhibition **13**
Opegrapha **52-3**; *O. vulgata* **52**
Ophiostoma novo-ulmi,
see Dutch elm disease
Orbilia comma **61-2**
Orkney **44,** *139*
Oughtred, Iain **45**
Oxyporus populinus **58**

Pachyphiale **52**; *P. fagicola* **53, 54**
Pannaria conoplea **54**
'Paradisiac Elm' **35**
Parmelia sulcata **51-2**
Parmeliella **52**; *P. testacea* **53**
Parmelina pastillifera **52**
Partridge breast **14, 45**
Peace, Dr Tom **66**
Peltigera **52**
Peniophora **59**; *P. cinerea* **59**;
P. incarnata **59**; *P. lycii* **59**
Perth **24**
Pertusaria albescens **51**
Peterken, George **28**
Phaeophyscia **51**
Phaeostalagmus tenuissimus **65**
Phanerochaete sordida **59**
Physcia **51**; *P. aipolia* **16,** *52*;
P. leptalea **52**; *P. stellaris* **52**
Physconia **51**
Phytophthora **65**; *P. cambivora* **65**;
P. kernoviae **65**; *P. ramorum* **65**
Piccolia ochrophora **52**
Pierpont Johnson, C. **40**
Pinus sylvestris **14**
Pipe manufacture **40-2,** *41*
Plant Health Act 1967 **67**
Platychora ulmi **61**
Pleurosticta acetabulum **54**
Pleurotus cornucopiae **57,** *57*;
P. ostreatus **57,** *62*
Pliny the Elder **37**

Pluteus **60**; *P. salicinus* **60**
Pollarding **26**
Pollen **17, 23-6,** *24*
Polyporus durus **59**; *P. leptocephalus* **59**;
P. squamosus **57, 58**
Porina **52**; *P. rosei* **53**
'Princess, The' **32**
Pseudocyphellaria **52**
Pyrenula hibernica **53**
Pythium intermedium **65**

Quarantine measures
    Dutch elm disease **69**
Quaternaria dissepta **61**

Rackham, Oliver **27-8**
Radulomyces confluens **59**
Raeburn, Sir Henry *40*
Ramalina **52**; *R. canariensis* **52, 54**;
R. farinacea **52**; *R. fastigiata* **52**;
R. fraxinea **52**; *R. lacera* **52**
Ramonia **52**; *R. chrysophaea* **53**;
R. dictyospora **53, 54**
Ratho, Edinburgh **73**
Red Data Book categories,
lichens **53**
Regeneration **17**
'Remarks on Forest Scenery, and
other Woodland Views' **12, 20**
Reproductive biology **28**
Resupinatus **60**
Rhizoctonia solani **65**
Rhodotus palmatus **56-7,** *56*
Richard, Rev Timothy **48**
Richens, Dick **15, 22, 34-5, 48**
Rigidoporus ulmarius **56**
Rinodina griseosoralifera **54**
River Helmsdale, Highland *8*
Robertson, Stanley **84**
Root diseases **65**
Rope making **47**
Ross, Angus **126-7, 134**
Ross-Craig, Stella *12*
Rot resistance **14, 40-3**

St Clement's Church,
Rodel, Harris **31**
St Cuthbert's Church,
Edinburgh **23**
St Fillan's Day **36**
St Monan's, Fife **41**
Sarcoscypha austriaca **62**
Schizopora paradoxa **59**
Schwarz, Marie Beatrice **72**

Sclerophora pallida **53**; *S. peronella* **53**
Scolytus multistriatus **68**; *S. scolytus* **68**
Scott, Sir Walter **32**
Scottish Arts Council **79, 144**
Scottish Borders **32,** *36,* **38, 47,** *64,* **76**
Scottish Highlands **68**
Scottish Natural Heritage **79, 84, 144**
Scottish Trees programme **78**
Scroggies Brae, near Carlops,
Scottish Borders **28**
Seiridium intermedium **61**
Shipbuilding **14, 45**
Sileas na Ceapaich **32-3**
Skeletocutis nivea **59**
Skye **45**
Soils **27**
'Species Plantarum' **21**
Spens, Dr Nathaniel *40*
Sphaerostilbe aurantiaca **62**
Splanchnonema foedans **61**
Stead, Tim **14, 46,** *46,* **87**
Stereum **58**; *S. hirsutum* **58**;
S. rugosum **58**
Stevenson, Savourna **81-2,** *82*
Sticta **52**
Strymonidia w-album **16,** *16*
'Stygian Elm' **35**
Suckering field elm **22-3, 28**
Sutton **62**
Swanney, Sandra **82**
Swift, David **128-9, 134**

Taliesin **34**
Tatton Park, Cheshire **13**
Tennyson **32**
Thelopsis rubella **52**
Theophrastus **21**
Thompson, Maurice **41**
Tierney, Lawrence **83**
Toaig, Peter **137**
Trametes **59**; *T. versicolor* **59**
Tree Council **72**
Tremella indecorata **60**
Tubercularia vulgaris **61**
Tyloses **69**

UK Biodiversity Action Plan **53**
UK Red List
    lichens, status **53, 54**
Ulmus americana **18**; *U. campestris* **21**;
U. folio latissimo scabro **21,** *21*;
U. minor **22-3**; *U. plotii* **22**;
U. procera **22,** *75*; *U. rubra* **37, 48**

United States of America **18, 65**
'Useful Plants of Great Britain,
The' **40**
Uses of elm **40-8**
Ustulina deusta **58,** *58*

Verticillium, albo-atrum **66**;
V. tenuissimum **65**
Vines
    connection with **35, 75**
Volvariella bombycina **57,** *62*;
V. volvacea **57**

Wadden-Holmes, Anastasia **80**
Wadeana dendrographa **53**;
W. minuta **52, 53**
Walker, Stephanie **80**
Walters, Mary **78, 83**
Waterpipes **14, 42**
Waterwheels **14, 42,** *42*
Watling, Roy **137**
Watt, Jennifer **130-1, 134**
Weather boarding **43**
Websites **141**
Western Highlands and Islands **53**
Westminster, Duke of **43**
Wheel making **14, 43-4,** *43,* **44**
White-letter hairstreak **16,** *16*
Wildlife and Countryside Act
1981 **53**
Wildlife associated with elm **15**
'Wildwood: A Journey
Through Trees' **18**
Wilt diseases **65**; *see also* Dutch
elm disease
'Witch's broom' **24**
Windsor chair **45**
Witchcraft **32**
'Witchery of Archery, The' **41**
Witches Tree **32**
'With the Grain' exhibition **46**
'Woodland Crafts' **42**
Woodland Trust **76**
Wych Elm Project **13-4, 76**
    community projects **77-84**
    exhibition, artists **85-131**

Xanthoria **52**; *X. polycarpa* **17**
Xanthorion communities **17, 51**
Xylaria hypoxylon **61,** *61*

York **24**
Yorkshire Dales **73**
Yurts **80-1,** *81*